SUBTLE

ENERGY

TECHNIQUES

Cyndi Dale

(Minneapolis, MN) is an internationally renowned author, speaker, healer, and business consultant. She is president of Life Systems Services, through which she has conducted over 65,000 client sessions and presented training classes throughout Europe, Asia, and the Americas. Visit her online at CyndiDale.com.

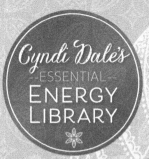

Cyndi Dale's
--ESSENTIAL--
ENERGY
LIBRARY

SUBTLE

ENERGY

TECHNIQUES

CYNDI DALE

Llewellyn Publications
WOODBURY, MINNESOTA

first edition
Fifth Printing, 2022

Book design by Rebecca Zins
Cover design by Ellen Lawson
Interior illustration on page 33 © Mary Ann Zapalac
Interior illustrations on pages 38, 105, 126 © Llewellyn Art Department

Llewellyn Publications is a registered trademark
of Llewellyn Worldwide Ltd.

Library of Congress Cataloging-in-Publication Data
Names: Dale, Cyndi, author.
Title: Subtle energy techniques / Cyndi Dale.
Description: First edition. | Woodbury : Llewellyn Publications, 2017. |
  Series: Cyndi Dale's essential energy library ; #1 | Includes
  bibliographical references.
Identifiers: LCCN 2016059606 | ISBN 9780738751610
Subjects: LCSH: Energy medicine. | Healing.
Classification: LCC RZ421 .D353 2017 | DDC 615.8/52—dc23 LC record
available at https://lccn.loc.gov/2016059606

Llewellyn Publications
A Division of Llewellyn Worldwide Ltd.
2143 Wooddale Drive
Woodbury, MN 55125-2989
www.llewellyn.com

Printed in the United States of America

Table of
-CONTENTS-

● ● ● ● ● ●
CHAPTER ONE
*The Energy of All
Essential Practices*   13

● ● ● ● ● ●

CHAPTER TWO

Of Intuition and Sources: Getting Ready for Energy Work 43

● ● ● ● ● ●

CHAPTER THREE

The Spirit-to-Spirit Technique 63

● ● ● ●

● ● ● ● ● ●
CHAPTER FOUR

Healing Streams of Grace   95

CONTENTS

● ● ● ● ● ●
EXERCISES

● ● ● ● ● ●
FIGURES

Disclaimer

The information in this book is not intended to be used to diagnose or treat any medical or emotional condition. To address medical or therapeutic issues, please consult a licensed professional.

The author and publisher are not responsible for any conditions that require a licensed professional, and we encourage you to consult a professional if you have any questions about the use or efficacy of the techniques or insights in this book. References in this book are given for informational purposes alone and do not constitute an endorsement.

All case studies and descriptions of persons have been changed or altered so as to be unrecognizable. Any likeness to actual persons, living or dead, is strictly coincidental.

INTRODUCTION

I've been studying energy work for nearly thirty years—and practicing for almost that long. I've assisted at least 65,000 clients and logged time learning and teaching in countries such as Japan, Morocco, Wales, Peru, Belize, Costa Rica, Iceland, and Russia, among others. I can't imagine doing anything else for a living, but I can whole-heartedly say, "I wish I knew *then* what I know *now*."

What if I had always used my now-signature technique called Spirit-to-Spirit? Maybe I wouldn't have ended so many work days drained, exhausted, and reverberating with my clients' physical pain and heartaches. Perhaps I would have offered more sage advice to the friend who needed it or spent less time muddled in decision making.

What if I had developed the technique called Healing Streams of Grace sooner? Perhaps that little girl with inoperable liver cancer might have enjoyed more pain-free time with her family or perhaps even still be alive. Maybe I would have enjoyed my trips to the mall instead of leaving with worries about the people who I sensed were in need of help.

The list goes on and on. I'm super happy that I can now use my Light Wand technique to relieve my own and others' stress and tension. I'm glad I'm able to help people access natural elements to create instant calm or energy. And as you'll discover in this book, I employ several other techniques to accomplish everything from repairing psychological wounds to accessing spiritual guidance. Overall, however, my greatest wish is that I'd developed these powerful concepts and techniques sooner.

While I can't turn back the clock in my own life, I can save you time and effort. That's the goal and gift of this book, as well as the other forthcoming books in my Essential Energy library.

Within this book, which kicks off the series, I share the most potent practices I've developed, adapted, and applied as an energy worker, or as someone who works with "moving information," during my nearly thirty years on the job. Energy work capitalizes on the fact that everything in the world, seen and unseen, is made of energy. It also acknowledges that there are two basic types of energy: subtle and physical. Subtle energy is immeasurable and underlies the more concrete physical energy. If you shift the subtle energies holding a physical problem in place, you have a far greater chance of altering material reality than if you only address the concern physically. Likewise, by opening to joy, health, and love on the subtle levels, physical reality can more quickly and permanently reflect these desires.

In these pages I explain and explore my energy-based techniques in-depth, fleshing them out with case studies and suggestions for application. Those of you who are familiar with some of my other books will notice that several of the techniques and concepts were first revealed elsewhere. I repeat concepts such as knowledge about chakras and intuition because these ideas are vital for the practices. None of my previous books, however, present the techniques in the same depth as within this one. In fact, one of the most constant requests I receive from readers is that they want a more thorough explanation of my go-to techniques. When teaching live classes I can accommodate this need. Before now, however, I haven't had the "ink space" necessary to thoroughly examine and outline my signature techniques. As well, I also share a variety of ways to conduct these techniques so that you can customize them to your own personality and needs.

Every technique can be used in any capacity of your life, personally or professionally, and can be shaped to

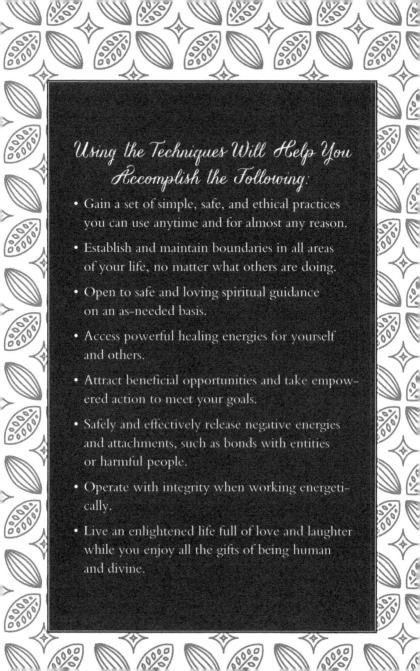

Using the Techniques Will Help You Accomplish the Following:

- Gain a set of simple, safe, and ethical practices you can use anytime and for almost any reason.

- Establish and maintain boundaries in all areas of your life, no matter what others are doing.

- Open to safe and loving spiritual guidance on an as-needed basis.

- Access powerful healing energies for yourself and others.

- Attract beneficial opportunities and take empowered action to meet your goals.

- Safely and effectively release negative energies and attachments, such as bonds with entities or harmful people.

- Operate with integrity when working energetically.

- Live an enlightened life full of love and laughter while you enjoy all the gifts of being human and divine.

assist you physically, psychologically, and spiritually. They can also be adapted to help (or cope with) all sorts of people, including yourself, loved ones, coworkers, clients, and children. They can even be employed for animals and other life forms, such as plants and trees, as well as the deceased and otherworldly.

How can a handful of techniques accomplish so many goals? The techniques in this book reflect four cornerstones, or pillars of truth that serve as a key focus for humanity, in the following ways:

HISTORY: Every technique is rooted in an established cultural tradition and frequently displays concepts found in most of the mystical societies.

Science: The efficacy of these practices can be explained in terms of energy and are therefore anchored in scientific theory.

Spirituality: The processes assume a Higher Power, no matter the name used. In this book I employ the term Spirit, but you can substitute one of your choosing: God, Allah, the Universe, the Creator, the Great Spirit, the Divine, the Holy Spirit, the Goddess, the Christ, the

Beloved, or even the Goodness of Humanity. The techniques in this book will work regardless of your religious or spiritual beliefs, as they are a summation of the highest sources of wisdom we can understand.

INNOVATION: It's important to recognize that we live in a different time period than our ancestors did. Because of this, I've updated the techniques rooted in history. We face different challenges now, such as the constant barrage of noise, too many emails, and electromagnetic pollution. Included in the latter category are the effects of invisible waves of energy such as from Wi-Fi, cellular communication, and the blue light emanated from devices including computers, cellular phones, and televisions. In fact, the latter causes so many disturbances in our mental stability and sleep that researchers are coming up with new filtering products, such as light bulbs and eyeglasses that screen out the unhealthy blue light. The fact that I've shaped techniques to make them contemporary and apply them to current stresses means that you can further adapt them to your unique self.

In terms of the mechanics of this book, the first two chapters serve as appetizers for the remaining chapters, which constitute the main course. In chapter 1 I briefly explain how energy works. I also share basic information about the chakras, which are one of the three main subtle energy structures that compose all living beings. You'll frequently be shown how to apply the techniques to the chakras, which affect change on every level simultaneously—physically, psychologically, and spiritually. Why not go for faster and easier change, which the chakras promise?

In chapter 2 I present two additional concepts: intuition and sourcing. It's necessary to understand these ideas if you're to perform the essential energy techniques featured in this book. In regard to intuition, there are four main intuitive styles, in addition to a catch-all category. After learning about these styles, you'll be able to more easily conduct the book's exercises, most of which employ intuition.

I use the term *sourcing* to acknowledge that there are many sources of information and assistance. The art of assessing and opening to sources of information makes a great verb. Some sources are good; others are harmful. Some are concrete and others are otherworldly. It's important to have a sense of these sources, as many of our life problems are caused by connections with sources of information that are harmful rather than beneficial. Conversely, receiving assistance from positive sources can jump us light years ahead, especially in terms of healing and manifesting.

From a subtle energy point of view, the negative connections are often held in place by invisible fetters called attachments. Throughout the exercises you'll be shown a variety of ways to free yourself from these chains of bondage.

At this point we get busy. Each of the subsequent chapters features a different signature exercise. The following synopsis of the techniques is meant to tempt you with the menu:

SPIRIT-TO-SPIRIT: This is an all-inclusive process for safely accessing information as well as performing healing, manifesting, prayer, meditation, and more. It also establishes energetic boundaries and assures only the highest outcome, no matter the request. Spirit-to-Spirit is a stand-alone technique, and you'll be shown several ways to use it in chapter 3. It also serves as the foundation for the other techniques in the book, each of which starts with Spirit-to-Spirit.

HEALING STREAMS OF GRACE: This technique can be used in any situation requiring change, transformation, healing, or a release from negative sources or issues. Like Spirit-to-Spirit, this process can be used independently or also in concert with the other techniques in this book. It will be referenced in almost every chapter after it's introduced in chapter 4.

TRANSFORMATION THROUGH THE ELEMENTS: I work with eleven subtle elements. These compose the natural elements that make up physical reality. Understanding the various ways to work with these subtle elements can accomplish nearly every goal, from clearing negativity to energizing the body. Though presented in chapter 5, the elements will pop up in several subsequent chapters.

THE LIGHT WAND: This simple technique, showcased in chapter 6, uses a finger to compel energy to enter or leave a problematic area, such as a body part or a subtle energy center.

IN-BODY JOURNEYING: This is an incredibly safe method for visiting other times and places to gain insight, information, and healing energies. Most other out-of-body journeying or soul-traveling techniques leave you vulnerable to negative forces. Discussed in chapter 7, this simple process will show up again in the subsequent chapters.

THE THREE SOUL RECORDS: The soul is like a recording studio with three main libraries within it. Accessing these three soul records is critical to recovering from past injuries and misperceptions, healing regrets and resentments, and perceiving reality through your divinity. After learning about these records in chapter 8, you'll be encouraged to use your knowledge of them in chapter 9.

TRAUMA AND AUTOIMMUNE RECOVERY: By tracking forces and releasing unhealthy bonds, you can help yourself or others recover from both trauma and self-induced destructive patterns. The exercises addressing these issues in chapter 9 will draw upon teachings from previous chapters.

THE FOUR SOUL ZONES: Before every incarnation the soul passes through four zones, or stages. Understanding these zones, the subject of chapter 10, is the key to altering your destiny, releasing past life memory blocks and negative attachments, reducing pain, energizing the body, and moving into a state of forgiveness and enlightenment.

It's now time to finish preparing yourself for the adventure ahead. Let us walk through the doorway of wisdom and discover what lies within your greater self!

CHAPTER ONE

The Energy of All Essential Practices

Years ago, Einstein's theories revealed that everything is made of energy. The scientific community could suddenly explain why ancient practices that employed divination, prayer, meditation, intuition, and various forms of holistic healing could so often create amazing and even near-miraculous results.

Energy is everywhere and composes everything. It flows from one state and place to another, constantly transforming, and can't be destroyed. And because we—and everything else—are made of energy, we are all connected, influencing each other with every thought, word, and deed. Because of the interconnected nature of energy, a slight shift in the subtle energies underpinning a physical reality can bring about a huge change in the concrete world. Even better, these changes can be brought about with activities as simple as adopting a new belief or perception, rethinking a decision, or following an intuitive hunch.

I'm not relaying a science lesson simply to present data. Instead, my goal is to support you in using the techniques in this book as boldly and frequently as you desire. That is why, in this chapter, I'm going to help you understand the nature of energy. This will help you better access your innate capacity to transform reality. From there, you can more easily steer your life toward joy and health and into loving relationships.

In order to meet this objective, I begin this chapter with an exploration of the essence of energy. I then proceed with a discussion about the differences and similarities between two basic types of energy, physical and subtle, showing you why the techniques in this book are oriented toward enabling you to tap into subtle energies. Then, finally, I introduce you to a very special subtle energy structure, the chakras. I will also familiarize you with the chakras' "kissing kin," the auric field. These two systems, especially the chakras, will be referenced frequently here.

As you acquaint yourself with the basics of energy, remember that you've been interacting energetically your entire life. At some level you are already an energy expert. More knowledge can only assist you in becoming a full-on master of energy—and, therefore, a master of your personal destiny.

Everything Is Energy
WHAT THIS MEANS FOR YOU

When I took physical science in eighth grade, I was informed that the world is made of matter. I was also told that although matter could change form, as water does when converting from ice to vapor to fluid, it was measurable and predictable.

At that time I didn't know if this explanation of reality should make me feel reassured or imprisoned. On one hand, the assurance that physicality was predictable gave me a sense of security. If I put a glass of water on a table, it would stay put unless I moved or smashed it. I could philosophically count on a world in which outcomes were foreseeable. On the other hand, if reality was completely meted out and constant, the ability to transform what I *didn't* like seemed pretty limited.

During the last few decades, science has debunked the notion that the world is staid and static. It turns out that the universe isn't actually made of matter. Rather, it's crafted from energy. Not only that, but energy isn't ever concrete or solid. Nothing stays in place, nor is it ever still. Energy constantly vibrates and moves. That glass on the table? The one that seems so handy? It's merely an illusion (Walia, "Nothing Is Solid").

Every component of that glass is shifting around, and many of the subatomic members of that glass aren't even anywhere near it. Sure, you can use the glass, but it turns out that this is because there is some sort of "agreement" (which I'll discuss in the next section in regard to subtle energy) making sure you can.

Why is it so important to know that energy is king? Every technique in this book carries the potential to better your life because the world is made of continually shifting energies, not substances stuck and immobile. Think of it. It's far easier to move a branch lying on the ground than a tree trunk stuck in the dirt. Nothing is really stuck in place, and that list can include a tumor, a bad job, or an emotional disorder.

Because energy is information that moves, there are two basic "handles," or characteristics, you can grab when you want to create change: information and vibration. Let's first look at the information component of energy. Information is the data that tells something to be itself. The information in the cells and particles related to a glass enable it to look like—and be used as—a glass. Within the human body, the information regulating it might be memories or aspects of our soul and mind (Pearsall 11–14). In addition, our surroundings inform our body, shaping what becomes of it. A simple example of this is the effect of sound and color on our health. It's been shown that too much noise and glare create stressors that can negatively affect our biochemistry, lowering our immune system and making us feel sad and depressed (Center for Spirituality & Healing, "What Impact Does the Environment Have on Us?"). We are incredibly open systems, constantly reacting to the information inside and outside of us.

The implication of energy being information is incredible. In terms of your own life, it means that you can insert different information into the formula creating a problem and thus potentially shift the problem. You can also support or bolster the information underlying a desire and more easily call it into being. For instance, imagine that you can't get a raise because your parents taught you that wealthy people are greedy and evil. If you debunk that belief, perceiving it as untrue, you free yourself from its power. Your attitudes, actions, and entire aura transform. You can now attract and respond to more fortunate opportunities. Furthermore, by inserting a new belief into your system, such as recognizing that a financial improvement would benefit you and your loved ones, you can really spread your wings. You can position yourself to receive a raise or apply for a new job with greater rewards.

The other characteristic of energy is vibration, or movement. As implied, information keeps any number of recognizable or material ingredients interacting long enough to create the semblance of permanence. But as concrete as an object or event might seem, it's not. All atoms are in constant movement. In fact, the atoms formulating any physical substance are actually linked by vortices of energy swirling in continual spin. These vortices are made of subatomic particles that dash from place to place, even in between dimensions and time periods (Walia, "Nothing Is Solid").

For the seeker of positive change, the fact of energy as vibration is exciting. In a nutshell, if you alter vibration, you alter reality. Break up or reassign the mini vortices holding specific atoms together, insert different vibrations, and you could potentially transform a lethal microbe into a benign one, disintegrate a tumor, attract that longed-for love, or accomplish just about any other goal.

Does this statement seem unrealistic? It's not. Consider the strange and lovely word *cymatics*. Cymatics is the study of sound and vibration made visible. In general, cymatic studies show that different sounds, which are composed of vibrating frequencies, generate different shapes. For instance, if you chant a specific tone over a plate of sand, a certain geometrical pattern appears. If you change tones, which involves altering the vibration, a different pattern forms (Cymascope, "Introduction"). You can modify vibrations enough to alter the appearance of sand, and the same can certainly be accomplished with other substances.

The art of altering energy is called *energy work.* In general, energy work is performed to activate or direct energy toward an optimum result. Energy work has been a foundation in countless cultures across time, just known by different names. You might better recognize the other terms used, such as faith healing, hands-on healing, shamanistic healing, chakra balancing, holistic therapy, spiritual healing, prayer, meditating, integrative medicine, alternative medicine, Eastern medicine, energy medicine, and the like. Because everything is made of energy, we could even say that eating a healthier diet is a form of energy work, as is undergoing surgery, taking prescription medicines, or exercising at the gym.

This book contains techniques that show you how to be an energy worker for your own or others' well-being. Does that mean I'm going to give you a list of preferred foods or behaviors? No, although I absolutely recognize the importance of taking real-life action to improve your life. Instead, the energy work techniques in this book are focused on helping you shift a particular type of energy to create more happiness, health, and prosperity. I call this energy *subtle energy*, and I'd like to explain it to you.

Subtle and Physical Energies
Why "Go Subtle"?

We've established that everything is made of energy, which is information that moves. These two characteristics are true of all kinds of energy. Energy further breaks down into two types of energy: subtle and physical energies. Knowing the differences and similarities between these energies will help you understand the reasons for using the techniques in this book, which are aimed at interacting with subtle energies.

Physical energies are those that appear solid and concrete. Their actions have traditionally been explained through the lens of classical physics. Sir Isaac Newton, one of the founding fathers, would basically have insisted, "What you see is what you get." In this worldview our oft-referenced glass remains on the table until it's picked up or broken.

Subtle energies are deemed invisible and immeasurable. Miracles, telepathy, psychic activity, spiritual awareness, and other mysterious events are usually attributed to subtle energies. These are the hard-to-describe energies that transcend time and space, let us talk with the dead, and experience all forms of intuition and mysticism.

Subtle energy has been assigned dozens of names over the centuries. It has been called *vril*, *shakti*, and *prana* in Hinduism, *hasina* in Madagascar, *pneuma* in Greece, *mana* amongst Polynesians, *orenda* by the Iroquois, *waken* by the Lakota, *tummo* in Tibet, *ki* in Japan, and *chi* in China. Relatively recent scientists have assigned it labels like biomagnetism, bioplasma, orgone, od, deltrons, time density, biophotons, the bioelectromagnetic field, the biofield, torsion fields, and dark matter. Obviously, the idea of a miraculous super energy isn't anything new and is also ever-evolving.

Today most experts examine subtle energy through the lens of quantum physics, the study of the smallest bits of matter. These tiny subatomic particles are called quanta, and you met them previously when I described the vortices in between the atoms of a glass. Remember the so-called glass? It was glued together—and could be found anywhere at once—because of ever-shifting sub-atomic particles, or subtle and immeasurable energies.

Subatomic particles aren't visible. We can't technically see them, and yet they are there, operating in ways that are often called "spooky." This adjective has been assigned because the rules of quantum reality are as mysterious as the quanta themselves. Becoming acquainted with a few of the quirky by-laws of the quantum world will pinpoint the reason that the techniques in this book are powerful.

You see, we live in a quantum, or subtle, reality. Knowing a few of the quantum rules, those most applicable to our transformational efforts and expressed and explained in everyday language, will reveal the opportunities available to us. In short, three of the most vital quantum laws are these:

- Quantum particles act more like waves than discrete units.

- Everything and everyone that has ever been connected continues to remain interconnected and affect each other. However, quantum rules allow for loving disconnections and changes in the types of energy being exchanged.

- What you perceive consciously will help shape physical reality (Orzel, "Seven Essential Elements").

Why is it important that quanta operate like waves rather than particles? Unlike particles, which are distinct, waves interact and affect anything they touch. The easiest way to understand this is to picture a pebble thrown into water. The water responds immediately and interacts with the pebble, but also the fish, plant life, and more. Subtle energies, or quanta, are similar. If you make a tiny subtle change, whether in information or vibration, all kinds of changes ensue. Subtle energies ripple through space and time, and keep on rippling. In other words, it takes very little effort to potentially transform your life by altering the subtle energies rather than only struggling to alter the obvious physical energies.

Entanglement is the term used to explain the fact that once two objects, particles, or even people have intermingled, they continue to affect each other. Obviously, this law might affect you positively or negatively. If a friend on the other side of the world unexpectedly wins the lottery, you might, too. But if this friend is stricken ill, you might find yourself sick as well.

Essentially, we're all connected to everything and everyone else. Have you heard about six degrees of separation? It's the theory that you only have to contact six individuals through someone you know to link with anyone else in the world. In the subtle realm, you're similarly bonded to everyone alive—and anyone or anything they've ever been in relationship with, dead or alive, animate or inanimate. Not only that, but you can theoretically snap your finger and be immediately in touch with any of these beings or things.

One of my favorite studies proving this point was conducted by a team of physicists led by Juan Yin at the University of Science and Technology of China in Shanghai. This team assigned a speed to the communication between photons, or quantum wave-particles of light, that were separated after being linked. They examined the state of one photon and timed how long it took for a change to be reflected in its partner, which was about ten miles away. They asserted that the slowest speed of the communique was 10,000 times the speed of light (Emspak, "Spooky!").

In relation to the techniques in this book, you'll learn how to analyze your subtle connections to make sure that they are beneficial rather than harmful. You'll also learn how to only link with people or beings, which I'll call "sources" in chapter 2, who are guaranteed to be supportive. I've found that many of my clients' problems disappear when they clear out the negative bonds and open to only positive ones. This statement is an off-shoot of the second quantum law, which states that you are affected by—and produce effects in—everyone you are connected to. If you alter your own energy positively, you start picking up or sending out only beneficial energy. For instance, one of my clients was stricken with one condition after another, including fibromyalgia, arthritis, high blood pressure, and more. We discovered that through the subtle realms, she was bound to several deceased ancestors and was actually experiencing the maladies they'd undergone when alive. Once we lovingly released these connections, an activity enabled by many of the techniques in this book, my client recovered. She scarcely gets so much as a cold these days.

Finally, in terms of subtle energy, it's important to acknowledge that shifting subtle energy can frequently alter physical reality and even create a new and improved version of it. This statement relates to a quantum law that states that the observer affects the outcome. In fact, many quantum physicists suggest that an aspect of physical reality can only come into being if an observer *chooses* to have that aspect appear.

This observer is your conscious self. I define consciousness as "active and conscientious awareness." I use this definition for several reasons. First, we can't be conscious if we aren't aware. Of course, a person can be self-aware and care less about anyone else. This sort of selfishness has created misery on this planet. Many of our problems also are due to a sort of group consciousness agreement, a "meeting of the minds" or a compact between souls allowing cruelty, discrimination, and hatred. The truly conscious person therefore must be conscientious, or able to make decisions based on their conscience, the innate sensitivity to goodness. Finally, a conscious person (or being) must be able to act on their conscientious awareness, otherwise they are merely gazing at their own navel. Love, the goal of consciousness, is the highest of all goals. We are here on this planet not only to give and receive love, but to consciously create more love than is already here.

The main tool of the conscious person is intention, the ability to serve in the role of an observer affecting an outcome. Every technique in this book is designed to help you become a wise and conscientious observer for yourself or another. In most of the exercises you'll be setting an intention to cause a specific change. You do this by formulating a statement that supports positive change. This statement then steers subtle energies in order to create the highest possible outcome. Since subtle energies interpenetrate all levels of reality, including other times and spaces, to consciously first shift the subtle energies and then pay attention to physical activities is to empower change across the board.

One of the vehicles that enables the steering of subtle energies are the chakras. Chakras are multidimensional centers of power. They can be easily piloted with intention, or consciousness. In turn, the laser focus we direct through the chakras, especially using my techniques, will bring about the highest outcome for all concerned.

In order to familiarize you with these vessels, the next section presents a general overview of the chakras. It also outlines the twelve-chakra system I have developed and constantly use in my personal and professional life.

The Chakras
VEHICLES FOR TRANSFORMATION

Chakras are subtle energy organs, also called centers and bodies, that compare in many ways to the bodily organs. One of three members of a greater subtle energy anatomy, they partner with subtle fields and channels to manage subtle energies and, through them, the physical self.

Each of your physical organs manages a set of functions and is located in a physical site. In a similar fashion, every chakra governs a set of concerns and is anchored in the physical body. Because the chakras are subtle organs, however, they can relate to more than bodily concerns. They also interrelate with your mind, soul, and spirit. Because of this, they manage psychological and spiritual tasks in addition to physiological functions.

There are seven main in-body chakras, each anchored in a nerve plexus and associated with an endocrine gland. Simplistically, these seven in-body chakras operate and respond to the body parts in their vicinity. For instance, the first chakra, found in the coccygeal area and linked with the adrenals, corresponds to parts of the hip, coccyx, urogenital system, rectum, and, of course, the adrenals. The main seven chakras are located in the hips, abdomen, solar plexus, heart, throat, forehead, and the top of the head.

Most Western chakra systems feature these seven in-body chakras. There are dozens of cross-cultural systems, however, that include anywhere between three and hundreds of chakras. In addition to the seven in-body chakras, I work with five out-of-body chakras. Knowledge of these powerful chakras exponentially increases the ability to support progressive change.

These out-of-body chakras only loosely connect to the spine, but—like their seven in-body kin—are each anchored in an endocrine gland as well as an area of the body. As do the seven in-body chakras, the external chakras manage particular psychological and spiritual interests. And spiritually, each of the twelve chakras accomplishes specific intuitive functions. You'll learn more about these intuitive faculties in chapter 2.

As implied, one of the main reasons that chakras are vital to energy work is that they interact with your soul, mind, and spirit, in addition to your body. Your soul is the part of you that travels from existence to existence to gather wisdom and gain experience. Most likely this hasn't been your only incarnation. You've probably experienced several other earth lives and also dwelled upon different planets and within a variety of star systems. As well, you've existed in-between lives on various planes of existence. Your soul carries the memories from all of these experiences, as well as your conclusions about them.

These memories are anchored in your mind, a matrix, or energetic net, that stores information for your soul. It threads into a greater matrix, which some call the nexus. The nexus passes through all realms and dimensions and acts like a gigantic Internet, gathering and disseminating information.

You have two parts to your mind. Your non-local mind easily taps into the nexus to upload and download information. It's called "non-local" because it's not located in just one place. Linked to the nexus, it's actually everywhere at once. Your local mind is primarily composed of your brain and neurological system. While your local mind is intricately linked to your non-local mind, we're not trained to access the interdimensional nexus. As well, our dysfunctional beliefs, cultural prejudices, and other factors limit our ability to access the resources of the nexus. Chakras act like doorways into the nexus. Because of this, the techniques in this book will frequently encourage you to perform energy work through the chakras.

Ultimately, your soul originates many of your beneficial and harmful capabilities and beliefs. The sum total of your soul's experiences is called your karma. This Hindu word is nonjudgmental and recognizes that your soul carries all information with it, lifetime after lifetime, and also transfers this information into a body with every incarnation. Upon entering this lifetime, your soul's issues were programmed into your genetics, subconscious, and other influential parts. Many of your life challenges mirror the soul's karmic data. For instance, if you were hung in a past life because of your intuitive gifts, you might experience neck pain in this lifetime. Psychologically you might also resist activating your intuitive abilities, as you fear a repeat performance.

Many of the processes in this book will help you remember past or in-between life experiences and clear the karma that may be creating shame, fear, or challenges. You'll frequently interact with a chakra or several chakras to accomplish these goals.

The other important aspect of the self is your spirit. You'll learn more about this term and the various meanings of it in chapter 3. Basically, your individual spirit is your essential self, which is always giving and receiving love. All the techniques in this book are aimed at inviting a full embodiment of your spirit in your this-life self.

So that it will be easier to select a chakra to work with while performing a technique, or understand the one I'm recommending you use, I have included the following table on the twelve-chakra system. See figure 1 for an illustration of these twelve chakras as well as a general portrayal of the twelve auric layers that surround the body.

The table references the chakras by number. Described are each chakra's location, which refers to the associated bodily area and endocrine gland; color, which depicts the related electromagnetic frequency; physical, psychological, and spiritual functions; and the spiritual purpose, with a focus on the available intuitive insights.

Some systems assign different colors than I do to the sixth and seventh chakras, describing the sixth chakra as indigo instead of violet and the seventh chakra as violet instead of white. Many people prefer the alternative because it follows the rainbow spectrum, which is based on nature. As well, violet is commonly perceived as kingly and regal and a suitable color for the top chakra, which is the most spiritual of the chakras. Because of this debate, the table first lists the color I use and then the alternate color. Through the rest of the book, I'll use my preferred colors, but you can substitute a different color if you want.

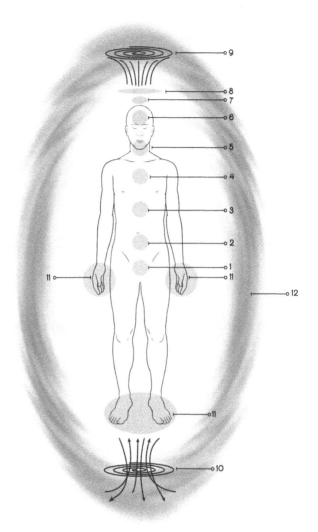

FIGURE 1: *The Twelve-Chakra System*

The Twelve-Chakra System

chakra	location	color	physical functions
First	Hips/ adrenals	Red	Governs hips, urinary and genital systems, the rectum, anus, and adrenals. Also manages all security needs, such as finances, career, sexuality, and life partnerships.
Second	Abdomen/ testes or ovaries	Orange	Manages ovaries, testes, intestines, and sacrum.
Third	Solar plexus/ pancreas	Yellow	Rules most digestive organs and digestive processes.
Fourth	Chest/ heart	Green	Manages functions of the heart, lungs, breast, and arms.
Fifth	Throat/ thyroid	Blue	Interacts with the throat, ears, mouth, jaws, and teeth.
Sixth	Forehead/ pituitary gland	Violet/ indigo	Linked to eyes, sinuses, hormones, and pituitary gland.
Seventh	Top of head/ pineal gland	White/ violet	Associated with higher brain functions, pineal gland, sleep, and mood.

psychological themes	spiritual purpose
Deservedness and worthiness; the right to exist and thrive.	Physical empathy. Empathic ability to sense what's occurring outside of the self in one's physical body.
Creativity. Rules feelings and our sensual and emotional expression.	Emotional empathy. Ability to empathically sense others' emotions within the self.
Willpower. Runs our belief system, affecting our self-esteem and self-confidence, and matters of power and work success.	Mental empathy. Empathic ability to know others' thoughts and motivations.
Love. Regulates exchanges in relationships involving self, others, and Spirit.	Relational empathy. Ability to relate to others with love. Also the center of healing.
Communication. Controls issues related to self-expression and all forms of verbal communication.	Verbal gifts. Ability to intuitively hear and express verbal messages.
Strategy. Monitors self-image and our long-term goals.	Visual gifts. Ability to intuitively perceive images, pictures, shapes, or other pictorial messages.
Spirituality. Determines connection between self and Spirit.	Prophecy. Our empathic ability to sense Spirit's will and carry it out.

chakra	location	color	physical functions
Eighth	Thymus. Is also an energy field located 1–2 inches above the head.	Black or silver	Linked to immune functions.
Ninth	Diaphragm. Is also an energy field found a foot over the head.	Gold	Governs breathing and oxygenation.
Tenth	Bones. Is also an energy field found a foot under the feet.	Brown	Runs bones and skeletal health, as well as our reactions to natural and inorganic substances.
Eleventh	Muscles and connective tissue. As an energy field, it is also concentrated around the hands and feet within the auric field.	Pink	Manages muscles and connective tissue.
Twelfth	Links to 32 points in the body. Is also found in the auric field.	Translucent	Regulates relationships between all parts of the body.

psychological themes	spiritual purpose
Karmic. Inserts our past and in-between life issues, feelings, and needs into this life.	Mysticism. Reflects our shamanic abilities to time travel and connect with spirits from all realms.
Idealism. Carries the ideals and spiritual laws we are supposed to live by.	Harmonizing. Carries all our soul's positive attributes and supports us in using them.
Ancestry. This center holds our ancestors' memories and serves as our link to nature.	Natural knowing. Allows us to communicate with ancestors and all beings of nature.
Connections. Manages our beliefs about connections and how to make use of them.	Commanding. Holds our ability to command natural and supernatural forces.
Spiritual. Holds our essential beliefs and qualities. If we activate this chakra, these higher truths can be programmed into the bodily self.	This chakra holds intuitive gifts that are unique to each person.

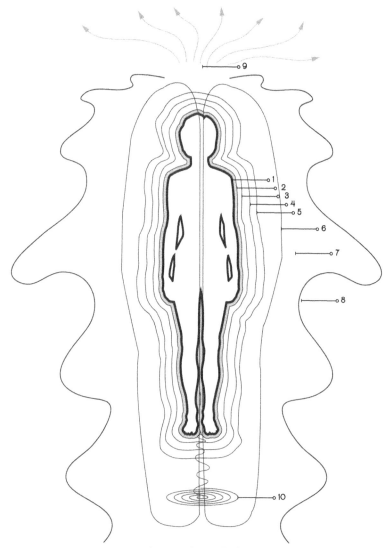

FIGURE 2: *The Twelve-Chakra Auric Field*

Your Chakras' Main Partners

THE AURIC LAYERS

Every chakra is partnered with one of twelve auric layers that compose the auric field, also called the aura. Overall, the auric field, or aura, is a set of subtle energy boundaries that assure safety through the filtering of subtle information. Specifically, each auric layer is an extension of a chakra and is the same color as its kin.

The job of the aura is to form subtle energy boundaries. These energetic boundaries screen incoming information and send information into the world, ultimately formulating the relationship you have with the external environment and everyone in it. Every layer is run by the information in its partnered chakra. This means that your first chakra, located in the hip area, manages the first auric layer, and so on. All auric layers "decide" how to purify and disseminate information depending on the programming in the related chakra. For instance, if your first chakra carries the belief that you deserve money, its related auric layer will attract money-making opportunities and supportive people. If the belief is the opposite, the layer might deflect prosperous situations or helpful individuals. Bottom line, you could say that the chakras manage the "you inside of you," and the related auric layers regulate the "you outside of you."

Several of the techniques in this book will reference the auric field. Because of this I would like you to be acquainted with the major twelve auric layers. As you can see in figure 2, the first auric layer emanates from the skin. Next comes the second auric field. From this point on, the auric fields encircle each other in numerical order, the third atop the second, the fourth atop the third, and so on. The eleventh and twelfth auric layers are not pictured but extend outward beyond the surrounding eighth auric layer.

Now that you have a sense of how energy works—and what energies are available for your use—it's time to learn the basics of intuition and sourcing. After chapter 2 you'll be ready to practice what's preached in this book.

* * * * * * *

Summary

Everything in (and outside of) this world is made of energy, which is information that moves. While subtle energies are immeasurable, they underlie physical energies, which are concrete and predicable. Energy work involves directing and managing subtle energies so you can better alter your everyday existence and create more joy, health, and love. Chakras and their partnered auric layers are subtle energy structures that can be accessed to work through the issues that lie in your soul, mind, or body and prevent the full expression of your spirit, which is your true self. The techniques in this book are aimed at enabling the embodiment of your spirit.

CHAPTER TWO

Of Intuition and Sources
GETTING READY FOR ENERGY WORK

In order to best direct subtle energies to your advantage, you'll need to understand two important concepts: intuition and the sources of subtle information. Equipped with this knowledge, you'll be able to improve matters by pinpointing the subtle energies creating your life challenges. You'll also be able to exponentially bolster the constructive aspects of your life and reach ever greater heights of spiritual awareness and joy.

Intuition is the primary tool for reading, assessing, interpreting, and directing subtle energies. Each of the chakras discussed in the last chapter is linked to a specific intuitive gift, or way of receiving and sending subtle messages. I organize these gifts into four basic styles—physical, spiritual, verbal, and visual—as well as a combined approach called the mystical style. By better understanding these styles, you'll more easily be able to implement the techniques in this book.

Sourcing is my term for describing the activity involved in analyzing the variety of sources of subtle energy information. Basically, there are worldly and otherworldly beings and groups that you can tap into for data as well as assistance. Sources can be helpful, neutral, or harmful. In this chapter I present a sample of the sources available for connection. I also describe the types of bonds that can keep people chain-linked to and victimized by negative sources. These bonds are called attachments, and there are many types. These will be succinctly explained in this chapter so you can free yourself from them in later chapters.

Now let's learn about intuition, the most vital vehicle for subtle energy transformation.

Intuition
YOUR "INTERNET ACCESS"

Intuition is the mindful management of subtle energy. There are intuitive faculties connected to each chakra, which I categorize into four fundamental styles and an additional combination style.

As you read through these main intuitive styles, pay attention to which you've used most often. You'll have ample opportunity to utilize your most developed skills and also activate additional ones when using this book's techniques.

Following is an explanation of the four main intuitive categories and the catch-all style. Besides describing the styles, I also highlight the related chakra.

Physical Intuition

Physical intuitives sense subtle energy empathically or kinesthetically, which means that they feel information in their bodies.

This style can be further subdivided into three subcategories:

PHYSICAL EMPATHY: If you're a physical empath, you sense others' bodily sensations in your own body, relating to people, animals, or other living or even otherworldly beings. You might also smell, taste, feel, or otherwise physically process information. FIRST CHAKRA

Emotional Empathy: If emotionally empathic, you sense others' feelings as if they were your own. SECOND CHAKRA

Mental Empathy: Through mental empathy, you know others' thoughts, beliefs, or motivations. THIRD CHAKRA

Spiritual Intuition

Spiritual empaths relate to subtle information through their spiritual awareness. Spiritual intuitives can be further divided into these subcategories:

RELATIONAL EMPATHY: Relational empaths respond to matters of love and relationship, knowing others' relational needs, hurts, and desires. FOURTH CHAKRA

Spiritual Empathy: If you're a spiritual empath, you ineffably understand others' spiritual desires and values. You might also ferret out areas of hypocrisy and understand another's life purpose and divine nature. SEVENTH CHAKRA

Harmonic Empathy: Do you "read" situations through bodily and spiritual awareness? You might be a harmonic empath, able to figure out what outcome is best, no matter the circumstances. NINTH CHAKRA

Force Empathy: If you're a force empath, you can command supernatural and natural forces. Supernatural forces compose the basis of sorcery and natural forces, including water, air, fire, and other elements. ELEVENTH CHAKRA

Verbal Intuition

If you are a verbal intuitive, you can hear words, songs, and messages in your "spiritual ear." You might also obtain verbal messages from the everyday world. For instance, a radio song might hold meaning for you. Verbal intuitives usually share intuitively received information to others through speaking, writing, singing, or the like. FIFTH CHAKRA

Visual Intuition

If you are a visual intuitive, you receive revelations that are psychically visual. The images can be packaged as colors, shapes, pictures, or even movielike dramatizations. Visual revelations might also pop in through the everyday world as well, such as on a billboard or a license plate. Many visual intuitives convey their intuitive insights through visual mediums, perhaps painting pictures or using imaginative words when talking. SIXTH CHAKRA

Mystical Intuition

If you are a mystic, you are basically a shaman, a "priest-healer" who uses all forms of intuition to receive information. Shamans can access various realms of existence to conduct interdimensional travel and connect with spirits. ALL CHAKRAS

As I stated, you'll use your intuitive faculties to conduct many of the exercises in this book. Intuition is also the key to performing yet another vital activity: sourcing.

Sources, Sources, and More Sources

When working with subtle energies, we absolutely have to ask this question: *To whom or what are you connecting to?*

This query is the basic one asked when *sourcing*, or determining the source of a subtle energy bond or message. Sourcing can also involve releasing negative sources and selecting uplifting ones.

In this book you'll be shown how to use your intuitive faculties to assess and choose sources. As a backgrounder, it's helpful to know that there are several basic classifications of sources.

On the most fundamental level, there are inanimate and animate sources. Inanimate sources aren't alive, but they can emanate energetic fields containing information. As an example, a treasured heirloom can be encoded with the emotions and memories of its previous owners. Grandma's rocking chair might still contain Grandma's wisdom.

Animate sources have self-awareness and consciousness. They might or might not be alive. For instance, you are an animate (and alive) source of information, as are the subcomponents of you, such as your body, mind, soul, and inner children, which are all the childhood ages you've experienced in this lifetime. You provide information to yourself but also to others. Other animate sources include living people, deceased people, and living and otherworldly animals, plants, and other natural beings. You can also connect to an aspect of another being, such as the inner child lodged in a friend or the infant aspect of your parent.

As stated at the beginning of this chapter, sources can be helpful, neutral, or harmful. Neutral sources don't hurt or help. Harmful sources cost energy or add disruptive energy. Helpful sources support the full embodiment of your spirit. These beneficial sources can also bolster your body, mind, or soul and help you help others.

The scariest sources are the negative or harmful ones. You might wonder how an inanimate source can be troublesome or deadly, but they can be—or, rather, the sources affecting these inanimate objects are problematic. Typically, a detrimental object or substance has been enchanted by an otherworldly or a living being.

The word *enchantment* evokes the image of spellcasting, which is exactly what I want to convey. A spell is simply a program containing subtle energy. A living or otherworldly being can "cast" a negative program into an object or substance either consciously or unconsciously. As an example, a favored piece of jewelry might inadvertently absorb the owner's hatred and cruelty. This energy can then be transferred into the next owner. And some people or otherworldly beings can deliberately "curse" an object so that inanimate object will continue to affect those connected to it, at least until the negative energy is released. (You'll be shown how to do that in this book.)

As an example, I own a silver pill box that was hexed by my Norwegian great-grandmother's childhood friend. Apparently my great-grandmother had "stolen" her friend's boyfriend. The friend had held the pill box and said something like, "May anyone who holds this get sick." (No one would believe that Norwegians perform their own version of voodoo!) From this point on, anyone who touched or carried the box experienced an illness right after. For instance, an uncle once played with the box and came down with a serious infection. When I first held the pill box when I was a child, I broke out in a rash. Eventually I used Spirit-to-Spirit (see chapter 3) and Healing Streams of Grace (see chapter 4) to clear the box. It's *really* an inanimate object now.

For the most part, the most abhorrent negative sources are animate. I usually use the labels "interference" and "dark forces" to describe the harmful sources that cause damage. The label "interference" illuminates the goal of the harmful source, whether it's worldly or otherworldly. Basically, a destructive source interferes with the life of its prey. The term "dark force" is pictorial. It emphasizes the way that interference works. In other words, interference darkens or overshadows the victim, almost as if to erase them.

Interfering discarnate beings are called entities. Disembodied souls may or may not ever have been alive. Ghosts are an example of entities that have once been alive. Still other entities have never been alive, such as angels and demons, which are described in the next section, "Types of Sources."

Interference is usually trying to achieve at least one of two goals. The first objective is to steal a victim's life energy. Life energy is the natural, physical, emotional, or mental energies that enable animation. Life energy is vibrationally dense and runs through—and is primarily manufactured within—the tenth, first, second, and third chakras. The second objective is to rob the victim of their spiritual energy. Spiritual energy is sent from the Spirit to a being. It enables enlightenment and growth. It can be pulled from the higher chakras, such as the fourth through the twelfth.

The most effective way for interference to steal life energy is to make someone feel scared, angry, hopeless, or powerless. Invisible entities cause these reactions by using subtle threats, speaking inaudible cruel words, or creating dilemmas in a person's life. They can even manipulate the people around a victim and set up scary situations. For instance, a dark entity might send a nightmare to a living person, implying that if they don't do X, Y, or Z, they will harm their loved ones. Living people manipulate in much the same way. They use shaming, blaming, and coercion to put others in a "one-down" situation and then take what they want.

Another goal of interference can be to trick a victim into giving up their connection to the Spirit's nourishment. Our personal spirits are constantly fed by the light of the Divine. The Spirit will never disconnect from us, but tricksters can convince us that we've been abandoned. Interference (usually otherworldly) might infer that we're evil, bad, or unworthy of the Spirit's love. If a dark force can convince us to turn away from the Divine's light, it can pilfer that light.

Beings or groups that want to permanently erase the spiritual connection between a victim and the Spirit are evil. Some beings become evil because they are so deeply unhappy that they want everyone else to fall into the same vat of despair. Others want to be as powerful as the Spirit. They steal the energy of their victims in order to gather power.

In order to differentiate between helpful and harmful sources, you need to know what types of sources exist. This is the topic of the next section.

Types of Sources

Following are descriptions of specific types of sources. It is a very thumbnail sketch; there are thousands of other sources of information. This information, however, will give you a starting place for deciphering the sources you'll search for in the techniques.

ANCESTORS: Many people or living beings remain anchored to earth after death, often bonding with their descendants. Members of a family line can help or hinder. For instance, I have a great-grandmother who was really psychic. She shows up in dreams every so often to help me develop my gifts. Yet another deceased ancestor downloaded his problematic emotions into me until I freed myself from him. He didn't want to deal with his emotions.

ANGELS/DEMONS: There are many types of angels, including archangels, seraphim, cherubim, and more. In general, beneficial angels deliver messages and assistance from the Spirit. The fallen angels (also called demons) steal life and spiritual energy and are frequently evil.

ANIMALS AND OTHER NATURAL BEINGS: Whether alive or in spirit form, animals and other natural beings—including trees, plants, rocks, and the spirits linked to elements—can serve as spiritual guides, deliver omens or portents, and convey healing and advice. Interfering natural beings can do everything from frighten you to cause disease. I've met many clients who continue to sense the presence of their deceased companion animals, and one client is actually visited by the spirit linked to a tree that had bloomed outside her window at her childhood home.

DECEASED: Anyone (or anything, such as an animal) that has existed before can be potentially

accessed, depending on availability or willing-
ness. This can include beings that lived on earth
or other realms, such as amongst the stars or in
other dimensions.

FAIRY REALM MEMBERS: There are many members
of the fairy realm, including fairies, dragons,
elves, unicorns, griffins, devas, and more. These
help grant wishes and tend to specific concerns.

MASTERS AND MORE: There are hundreds of high-
level and powerful beings. Some have incarnated previously and some have not. When
they aid us they are frequently called spiritual
guides. The short list includes saints, avatars,
masters, beings of the stars and planets, ascended
masters, extraterrestrials, and more. The dark
forces can also be avatars, masters, and as powerful as their beneficial counterparts.

Self: You can be your own source of information.
You can connect with your own inner children,
past life selves, in-between life selves, future
selves, and your mind, soul, or spiritual essence.

At this point, you might be wondering how interference remains connected once it latches on. Basically,

interference forms invisible yet potent energetic attachments. I examine this issue in the next section.

Energetic Attachments
HARMFUL BINDINGS

Energetic attachments are subtle energy bonds that bind at least two beings. Both or all participants are harmed by this linkage, but frequently one party is harmed more than another. For instance, if a mother attaches to her unborn child, the child usually ends up absorbing the mother's issues and problems. In return, the mother might receive the child's life energy. It might seem that only the child is being hurt, but the mother is preventing herself from maturing and being responsible. These attachments are formed from subtle energy but can cause physical, psychological, or spiritual effects.

An energetic attachment can anchor into any aspect of us, affixing into the soul, mind, or a part of the body. It can also enter through genetic material, be conjoined with an inner child, or screw into a chakra or set of chakras and the related auric layers. Attachments can also flow through the entirety of the auric field, in which case it takes complete control.

These attachments can exist between anything and anyone. You might be affected by an attachment to a deceased pet or a ghostly apparition. You might be linked to a fallen angel, a living parent, a friend, or an entire family system. As long as these energetic attachments are active, they limit joy, success, health, or access to love. This is because an attachment involves the loss of your life energy or spiritual light, for reasons described in the previous section. They might also serve as conduits through which another's unwanted energy flows into you. These incoming energies create intense problems, as we can't process energy that doesn't belong to us. While others' energies enter as subtle energy, this energy can be transformed through the chakras into physical or emotional energies and cause illness, emotional issues, or other blockages.

Several of the techniques in this book will help you lovingly and safely release or transform these types of bonds. Most frequently you'll use Spirit-to-Spirit from chapter 3 and Healing Streams of Grace from chapter 4. Following are descriptions of the main types of energetic attachments and an example of each.

Cords

These energetic tubules look like garden hoses coupling two or more beings. There is always an unhealthy exchange of energy inside of a cord. Through a cord, you can lose positive or life-enhancing energy, take in another's toxic energy, or experience both problems.

As an example, Jamie was a client with ovarian cancer and depressive feelings. There was a cord between her and her deceased mother. The cord attached to Jamie's second chakra and therefore anchored in her abdomen and ovaries. Through our work, Jamie determined that when her mother was alive, she had absorbed her mother's emotions—and was continuing to do so beyond the veil. After clearing the cord, my client underwent a hysterectomy and has been successfully clear of cancer for several years. Equally important, she feels happy and empowered.

Curses

These attachments are constructed from multiple cords. Psychically, a curse looks like a tangled mess of spaghetti noodles. Curses are forced upon someone or a group by another person, entity, or group. They hold the victims in bondage and cause disruption. They can be passed down within a family, be applied to a certain gender or a sub-group of a culture, or be carried in an individual's soul and reactivated during the start of each lifetime.

One of the more dramatic situations I worked with involved a family in which all the men who married into it died an early death. The mother of three grown daughters called me. She had lost several husbands, and her daughters had lost husbands as well. She reached out because one of her daughters wanted to remarry, and she wanted to stop the pattern.

We figured out that the curse had been placed on an ancestress who had spurned a lover in favor of another. The ex-lover threw a curse upon the woman that might be stated something like this: "Because you won't pick me, anyone you love will die." Since we lifted the curse using the techniques in this book, there have been no further losses.

Markers

These energetic contracts look like an *X* and might be etched over an auric layer, on a chakra, or over a body part. An energy marker is like a curse that tells others how to treat the affected person. For instance, I worked with a man who constantly attracted abusive male lovers. His brother, who had been jealous of my client's success as a jock and great student, had cast an energy marker over my client's heart whereby a potential lover was then subtly instructed to treat the man poorly. We removed the energy marker, and my client was soon in a loving relationship.

Miasms

A miasm is the product of a familial curse or set of psychological rules that makes sure everyone in the family supports the family system, no matter how unhealthy it is. It looks like a net intertwined in the auric field. The same matrix pattern is mirrored in all other family members' fields. When someone attempts to act differently than the family would desire, the net is "electrified" and punishes the rebellious.

As an example, alcoholic family systems are frequently enforced by a miasm. The miasm holds members in either an addict or enabler role. For example, I once worked with a sixteen-year-old boy whose parents brought him in to see me. They were deeply concerned about his addictive behavior, which included abusing alcohol and pot, amongst other substances. While both parents were sober, every one of their parents had been alcoholics. Sometimes miasms skip generations, which was occurring in this case. The young man had already been through several rehabilitation programs and insisted that something surrounded him that compelled him to act out.

This young man was willing to use the techniques in this book, including Spirit-to-Spirit and Healing Streams of Grace, and restart a twelve-step program. Within a few weeks he was sober. The best news is that he's been alcohol and drug free for five years and is finishing up college. In his words, "The net around me is gone." That "net" was the miasm.

Now that you are prepared to work energetically, it's time to learn the most important technique: Spirit-to-Spirit.

* * * * * * *

Summary

There are five major intuitive styles. The main styles, or "colors," of intuition are physical, spiritual, verbal, and visual. The fifth style is mystical and is a mix of the other four. Intuition is a vital tool for accessing and sharing information and will be used to perform the techniques in this book. It is also the key to sourcing, which involves assessing and selecting otherworldly and worldly sources of subtle information. Many of the negative sources are attached to their victims through attachments, such as cords and curses. In this book you'll learn how to spot and free yourself or others from these attachments and open to the spiritual guidance you truly deserve.

* * * *

CHAPTER THREE

The Spirit-to-Spirit Technique

The first time I taught my signature Spirit-to-Spirit technique to a large audience, a woman raised her hand and stated, "So, we could basically replace all our other healing techniques with this one?" I said, "Pretty much." I did add that my other signature technique, Healing Streams of Grace, would top it off.

As an energy worker, I begin every session with Spirit-to-Spirit. It creates a buffer between myself and a client, it supports the most optimum agenda and outcome, it guarantees I receive only accurate intuitive information, and it lets me leave the session behind when it's done. Spirit-to-Spirit is so universal that I've received rave reviews from members of all professions, including accountants, medical doctors, homemakers, veterinarians, speakers, farmers, and others. No matter the career, Spirit-to-Spirit establishes boundaries and activates the user's best self. It also allows the user to step aside and bring in a greater power while maintaining a sense of self.

Spirit-to-Spirit is equally empowering on the personal front. Even if you've only a split second to spare, you can access it to receive guidance, erect energetic boundaries, and reenergize. It's also an ideal (and quick) process for making decisions, dealing with a psychological trigger, and activating healing, among other activities.

I'm excited to fully introduce you to this technique because I've seen what it can do. To introduce you to Spirit-to-Spirit, I begin this chapter by showcasing the objectives achieved by this technique. I then present the technique's almost too-simple three steps. Finally, I present two Spirit-to-Spirit exercises.

The first exercise shows you how to conduct Spirit-to-Spirit when connecting with someone or something outside of yourself. You can use this exercise when speaking to a group, conducting a client or patient session, meeting with your mom, or even training your dog. It can be conducted with a goal in mind—or no specific objective. In case you know what goal you want to achieve, the exercise lets you build in a statement of intention, which is a focused desire.

The second exercise shows you how to use Spirit-to-Spirit for a personal reason or when alone. As with the first exercise, you can conduct Spirit-to-Spirit with a goal or without one. You'll be shown where and how to set an intention into the process, if you desire one.

An important part of Spirit-to-Spirit involves accessing your intuition, which we discussed in chapter 2. In the two outlined versions of Spirit-to-Spirit, I'll include a smattering of the four different ways of being intuitive, inviting you to practice each. I won't go overboard; I simply want to acquaint you more thoroughly with your own intuitive faculties. As we move deeper into the book, you won't be walked through the various styles literally but simply asked to trust whatever shows up intuitively.

Along the way, I'll continue to dole out stories that suggest a few of the hundreds of ways you can use Spirit-to-Spirit. Be creative! There are probably as many ways under the sun to use this technique as there are rays of the sun.

What Can Spirit-to-Spirit Accomplish?

Years ago I was searching for a single technique that could accomplish several goals. I was tired of using dozens of techniques to accomplish the following objectives:

- Establish energetic boundaries between myself and a client—or anyone else, for that matter.

No more ending the day feeling everyone else's emotions, illnesses, and dissatisfactions. No more meeting with a relative and ending up with their pains and problems. No more shopping at the mall and knowing too much about fellow shoppers.

- Invite only the highest agenda. I recognized that none of us know what's really best. I reached a point where I only wanted God's will to be done.

- Receive only beneficial spiritual guidance. Personally or professionally, I wanted to open intuitively to only the safest and godliest sources of information.

- Be protected from negative and manipulative influences, including dark entities, depressive attitudes, attachments, and overpowering "group energies" such as cultural, gender, ethnic, religious, or other discriminatory dogmas.

- Continue to develop personally. I was tired of my own psychological triggers. I wanted a continual transformation into more joy.

My search took me into dozens of cultures and places around the world. I studied with healers, shamans, and intuitives in jungles, deserts, islands, and mountaintops. I delved into thick and mysterious books; a few were hundreds of years old. Other tracts were small, tattered, and thin, probably only read by a handful of individuals. I attended a biblical seminary and participated in Lakota-style ceremonies. I learned how to perform Reiki, Therapeutic Touch, hypnosis, transpersonal psychology, Huna (Hawaiian) healing, and more. But I didn't feel any closer to discovering a single, simple, and elegant practice until one night when I had a dream.

In the dream I was told by guidance that there were only three steps necessary to accomplish the goals that I had set forth, and these were available for people regardless of their spiritual or religious beliefs, purpose, or training in healing or intuition. Then I was shown the three steps, which took all of a few moments to learn.

Stunned, I asked what I should call the technique. I was told to keep it simple. Since the three steps all involved calling upon a form of Spirit, I uncreatively called it "Spirit-to-Spirit."

Since using this process, I've seen that it meets all the goals I had set and more. It can be used when you are alone or with a group; when praying, meditating, speaking, teaching, or hanging out; and when seeking guidance or trying to control your temper. I use it constantly.

Next, I want to share the three steps of Spirit-to-Spirit. You might think they are too easy, but that's one of the reasons that they work. All truths are essentially simple.

The Three Steps of Spirit-to-Spirit

As stated, there are only three steps in the Spirit-to-Spirit technique. I'm going to describe each step, define the particular meaning of the word *spirit* used in that step, and state which goals are met by each step.

1: Affirm Your Personal Spirit

In this step, the word *spirit* refers to your unique spark of divinity. To affirm your spirit is to intentionally align your essential self with only the highest good. By doing this, you are assuming full connection with the Spirit, upgrading your personal and perhaps prejudicial agendas so they are of the highest order, and giving permission for Spirit to provide your more human self with healing and insight. You are also immediately provided the energetic boundaries needed for whatever task is at hand.

2: *Affirm Other Spirits*

In this step, the word *spirit* has two meanings. It refers to the divine essence of one or more living beings and also otherworldly beings.

The purpose of this step is to activate the divine spirit within others. In regard to the living, you don't have to be in their physical presence. You can silently affirm a friend when on the phone with them or simply focus on the subject.

Implicitly, when affirming another being or a group, you are also acknowledging the otherworldly beings linked to them, as well as yourself. We all have spiritual guides, which can include angels, the deceased, power animals, the souls of plants, or fairy beings, among others. When you acknowledge these spirits, you affirm that only the most transcendent can engage with your process. This activity filters out negative entities or dark forces. Know, too, that Spirit-to-Spirit can be performed when you are alone and focused on yourself. In this case, this second step involves affirming only your spiritual guides, as there aren't any concrete beings present.

Know that this step does not give you control over others. Others' personalities, issues, or needs don't disappear; instead, their best selves are brought forward. This action helps others transform manipulative agendas into positive ones and step away from interference that might be influencing them.

3: Affirm the Spirit

In this step, Spirit represents God, the Holy Spirit, Allah, the Greater Spirit, the Goddess, the Divine, the Greater God, or whatever term you might use for the Higher Power. This is the most critical of all three steps.

Performing this step is equivalent to surrendering your will to the Spirit's will. It allows your best self to partner with the Spirit to bring about the most optimum outcomes. It bolsters confidence in the intuitive information you receive and the actions you feel led to take. With this step, the Spirit provides protection for you and all others involved in a situation, and you can rest assured that all will be well.

Let me give you an example of how these three steps work.

An Example of Spirit-to-Spirit

One of my students is a massage therapist. Before learning Spirit-to-Spirit, she ended her working day completely exhausted, depressed, aching, and angry. She knew that she was absorbing her clients' pain and suffering, but she didn't know what to do about it. She was also scared that if she stopped taking on their energy, her clients might quit coming to her. "Maybe the only reason I'm a good massage therapist is that I take on their problems," she wondered.

I suggested that she start every session with Spirit-to-Spirit. She only needed to take a moment and she could perform it silently, quickly affirming her own spirit, the spirit of a client and all involved spiritual guides, and that of the Spirit. At this point she could conduct the massage, knowing that the Spirit was in charge of all aspects of the work.

My student glowed when she returned to class a month later. She shared that since using Spirit-to-Spirit, she hadn't absorbed clients' energies. "Not only that," she remarked, "but my intuition has exploded. I receive whatever empathic sense I need, and each client has reported improvement."

Next, I encouraged the student to use Spirit-to-Spirit in her personal life. At first she was nervous; her mother had been extremely religious—and mean. "I don't want to sound like a religious extremist," she reflected, wringing her hands.

I explained that Spirit-to-Spirit can be carried out as quietly in our personal lives as in our professional lives. She agreed to implement Spirit-to-Spirit whenever she was angry with her small son, who was three years old and a handful.

Yet another month passed and she returned to the class. Everyone wanted to hear her report. She disclosed that whenever her son threw a tantrum, she ran through a quick Spirit-to-Spirit. During the first couple of weeks, he continued with his full-blast explosions, but she didn't react. "Last week," she revealed, "he started a tantrum and then stopped and stared at me. Then we both started laughing."

As you can see, Spirit-to-Spirit benefits ourselves and others because we're held in bigger hands than our own. Do you want these same gains for yourself? I'll demonstrate the two exercises after showing how you can use your intuition to perform an affirmation. To be powerful, an affirmation has to be more than a cursory statement. A true affirmation deeply engages all aspects of ourselves toward an endeavor. Our intuition connects our body, mind, and soul. When we affirm a commitment to our spirit, others' spirits, and the Spirit through our intuition, we unify all aspects of the self within that goal.

Performing an Affirmation

How do you perform an affirmation? There is actually nothing to it. Most people don't believe me, however, until they experience the ease of affirming.

Another word for affirmation is recognition. To affirm a spirit, spirits, or Spirit, all we have to do is to recognize or acknowledge them. Acknowledgment can be done with any of the intuitive styles, which were presented in chapter 2. In the upcoming exercises I will frequently reflect ways to incorporate the different styles through each of the three main steps of Spirit-to-Spirit. The fifth style, the mystical, integrates these four approaches.

As a reminder, the intuitive ways of knowing are as follows:

PHYSICAL INTUITION: If you are a physical intuitive, you will sense truth in your body, recognized as physical sensations, emotions, or "knowings."

Spiritual Intuition: Spiritual intuitives relate to spirit/s or Spirit through the ineffable connection of love. Through the affirmation process, you might sense a loving presence or be filled with grace. You might be prompted to embrace your inner wisdom or be overtaken by a rush of wisdom. The end result is an awareness of unity.

Verbal Intuition: If you're a verbal intuitive, you have it easy: you don't actually need to sense something to create an affirmation. Simply state the affirmation. Aloud or internally, formulate a statement, such as "I affirm (my spirit/others' spirits/the Spirit)." If you want, you can write it down. You might also hear a guide or Spirit formulate the statement for you.

Visual Intuition: If you're a visual intuitive, I suggest you create an image that you can internally concentrate on when making an affirmation. Common examples include a light, lamp, or candle; a picture of the sun or a star; or the beaming of a bright light running through you. You can also employ a prop. A friend of mine has drawn the name of God in Arabic on paper and laminated it. She visually focuses on it to affirm the Spirit.

Mystical Intuition: You can use any or all of the above messages or develop your own approach. The other word I use to describe this blended intuitive form is shamanic. Shamans are priestly healers who employ all the spiritual gifts to access the various dimensions and planes of existence. If you are a mystical intuitive by nature, you are basically a shaman.

Spirit-to-Spirit
INTERACTIVE

This exercise shows you how to perform the three steps of Spirit-to-Spirit when interacting with another person, being, or group. You can enter the exercise with a goal or without one. If you desire a goal, you'll be shown where to set an intention or focused desire.

What if you want to focus on an exchange with something or someone that isn't physically around you? Perform the following version of Spirit-to-Spirit before a phone call or writing an email. You can simply imagine that the person is with you. You can also hold a picture of them or an object that represents your relationship, such as a piece of their jewelry or an article of their clothing, or write their name on a slip of paper.

Know, too, that it doesn't matter how many people you are going to associate with. Each is an individual. Imagine that the steps in Spirit-to-Spirit, especially the second step, will apply to everyone present. Neither does it matter if the interactions involve a non-person or a deceased person. You will conduct the three steps of Spirit-to-Spirit exactly as if associating with a person.

Now you can continue with your three steps, following a short preparation.

PREPARATION/INTENTION: Think about the being or beings you are going to interact or engage with. They may or may not be present. Take a few deep breaths and quiet yourself. You can conduct the next three steps internally. If you have a goal, shape it into an intention, such as "I would like to create this type of communication" or "I would like to accomplish XYZ."

Step One: **Affirm Your Own Spirit.** Focus on your chest area and acknowledge the fact that you are—and have always been—a divine light.

Sense, see, or internally acknowledge this shimmering light.

STEP TWO: **Affirm Others' Spirits.** Focus on the subject/s. Now affirm their spirit/s and then the otherworldly beings in attendance.

You might sense the goodness of these others in your body or become aware of the others' lovability and worthiness. If verbal, create a statement like this: "I acknowledge the vital goodness of everyone I'm engaging with, seen and unseen." If you are visual, ask to intuitively perceive the shine of the others' true spirits. If you are mystically gifted, you can use any or all of the intuitive faculties to affirm the others' spirits.

STEP THREE: **Affirm the Spirit.** This step involves turning the entire situation over to the Spirit.

Feel the presence of the Spirit. Acknowledge the Holy One's divine comfort, power, and grace. If you are verbal, make a statement, such as this: "The Spirit is now in charge of every aspect of this situation and all interactions." If visual, you might envision a dove, a white light, a rainbow, or the figure of Spirit you relate to, such as the Goddess, God, Kwan Yin, Mary, Christ, or Buddha. Allow the image to sweep through you and lift all burdens off your shoulders.

If you've established an intention before conducting Spirit-to-Spirit, know that during this step the Spirit will shape and form that intention so it reflects the best outcome for everyone. You can now interact with your subject/s as you desire. It is not necessary to close these steps, for the Spirit will continue to interact with you until you've finished the interaction and even beyond.

Extra Spirit-to-Spirit Tips

- After kicking off Spirit-to-Spirit, continue to pay attention to any guidance you receive, knowing it comes from the Spirit. Sense how the words you need to hear or speak simply flow through you. Pay attention to any images shared with you. Feel how you are able to keep your heart open, no matter how others are speaking or acting. If you feel triggered, confused, or overwhelmed at any point, take a deep breath and quickly perform step three again, turning over the management of the communication or activities to the Spirit.

- What do you do if someone else's goal differs from your own? Say you want to quickly get through a tax audit, but the auditor wants to spend a lot of time combing through your records. You can still set an intention for yourself before performing Spirit-to-Spirit. When the other's goal becomes clear, simply ask the Spirit to accommodate all goals. Sometimes it's unethical to support another person's objective. Perhaps they want you to help them bully someone else. Again, ask the Spirit to be in charge of the process, an activity which naturally occurs in step three, and follow where you are led.

Additional Insights and Scenarios
INTERACTIVE SPIRIT-TO-SPIRIT

Following are a few ways you can apply Spirit-to-Spirit when interacting with another (or others) and examples of the same.

Coffee with a Friend

How might this exercise look if you are having coffee with a friend? Before entering the coffee shop, take a moment and flip through the three steps. If you have a specific goal in mind, focus on it before you conduct step one, the affirmation of your own spirit.

What happens if your friend has a specific need that comes up during the conversation? You can actually conduct another Spirit-to-Spirit. Simply create a goal—such as "I'd like to know how to help my friend with this"—and affirm your spirit, your friend's spirit and her helping spirits, and the Spirit. Remember, you're turning the process and outcome over to the Spirit in step three and will be shown intuitively how to support your friend.

A Challenging Situation

What if you are walking into a troublesome situation? Spirit-to-Spirit is perfect for that scenario. Just use it; you don't even have to believe it will work. I'll give you an example.

Years ago I went to my aunt's funeral. I loved my aunt and her family but I struggled with one of my relatives, who I knew was attending. For years she had been extremely mean to me. She yelled when in person, gossiped behind my back, and in general acted frightfully.

I was shaking so badly when driving that my car wandered a bit. Sitting in the parking lot, I was sweating and my breath was shallow. With little faith in the process, I performed the three steps of Spirit-to-Spirit anyway. Before starting Spirit-to-Spirit, I simply asked to be the best person I could be at this event.

As I walked toward the front door of the funeral home, I sensed a swirl of spiritual support around me. I stopped quaking. I began to breathe deeply. Not only did I feel the Spirit, but also dozens of angels.

When I stepped into the lobby, I saw my angry relative. With complete composure I walked up to her, said hello, and told her that she looked beautiful. She was so stunned, she didn't yell! I felt calm throughout the entire event and ultimately did what I had come there to do: I honored my aunt's soul.

Professional Setting

Spirit-to-Spirit is a must-use in a professional setting, no matter your career. Here is a striking example of its power.

During a seminar I taught Spirit-to-Spirit to a police officer, who called me a few weeks later to relay a story. The officer was called to the home of an active domestic violence scene. He walked into a living room where a man was waving a gun around the room, pointing it first at his wife and then at his small son. The police officer had no idea what to do. He was new on the job and his mind went blank. After quickly performing Spirit-to-Spirit, he found himself talking to the gunman about the gunman's childhood. The gunman revealed that he had grown up in the projects and that his father had killed himself. Eventually the gunman laid down the gun, deciding he didn't want to continue his father's violent legacy.

The police officer swore that he only knew what to say because of Spirit-to-Spirit, which "sent words through" him. The keys to applying Spirit-to-Spirit in a professional setting include using it on the down-low, or secretly; in other words, perform it internally. Then trust that what you're led to say or do—or refrain from saying or doing—will help all concerned.

Dealing with a Group

Group energy can be wonderful. I love teaching classes because the individuals in the group usually work toward a higher purpose, asking questions that illuminate truths for every person in the workshop. But some group energies are puzzling or sticky, such as:

- The leader has an agenda not shared by the participants. For instance, the leader wants to figure out who to lay off and the group members want to save their jobs.

- Everyone but one person is on the same page. Frequently a group includes a rebel, that person who disagrees with everyone else.

- The group's agenda is at odds with that of a greater authority. For instance, a store wants all individuals to use whatever bathroom they are comfortable with, but the state government has gender-specific rules.

- The group is a "hard group." This all-too-common experience can apply to just about anything, from family reunions to mediation situations. There doesn't seem to be a winning solution, no matter what.

Of course, the intention you set depends on your position in the group. Are you the leader, participant, authority, dependent, or rebel? No matter what, run Spirit-to-Spirit and concentrate on step three. Remain in contact with the Spirit before, during, and for as long as necessary after the group experience.

Dealing with a Negative Person

Sometimes other people can be super challenging. Sometimes we're the challenging person. I always use Spirit-to-Spirit when I feel like I'm being mistreated, ignored, or defamed, or if I feel like doing something like that to another. As an example of dealing with a negative person, I once supported a client in using Spirit-to-Spirit with her mother, who was an extremely negative person. I'll call this client Maxine.

Maxine had undergone years of therapy to try to cope with her mother, who was gracious to everyone outside of the family but never to Maxine, who was an only child. Typical interactions ended with Maxine angrily stuffing her face with donuts and muffins, using the carbs to stifle her pain. Finally Maxine decided she would conduct Spirit-to-Spirit before talking or seeing her mother, no matter what.

The first few times that Maxine interacted with her mother, she reported feeling frustrated but noticed that she had stopped craving the carbs. After a few months Maxine found her mood unflappable, not affected by her mother's piercing criticisms. After about a year of using Spirit-to-Spirit, Maxine actually started to appreciate her mother's finer qualities, like her keen intellect and attention to details. Though Maxine didn't change, her attitudes did, as did her habits and patterns.

As might be expected, the key to employing Spirit-to-Spirit when interacting with a difficult person is to refrain from desiring change in the other person. If you're the one interacting with the Spirit, the Spirit has the greatest chance of making a difference with you.

Dealing with an Attachment or Entity

In my work I am constantly exposed to clients' dark forces and attachments. Once a client came to see me and said he was sure he had an entity attached to him. Immediately I established the intention of freeing him from the entity, conducted Spirit-to-Spirit, and felt the Spirit lift the entity off of him in step three. With situations like these, however, I usually also use Healing Streams of Grace, which are discussed in the next chapter, along with how to deal with entities and attachments.

Spirit-to-Spirit
PERSONAL FOCUS

Spirit-to-Spirit is a beautiful process to conduct alone or for personal reasons. It can help you ground, focus, and engage with your best self. It can link you with spiritual guidance, healing energies, and help you manifest. And it works whether you know what you need or not.

The most frequent question people ask when they want to perform Spirit-to-Spirit alone is how to perform step two, which involves affirming others' spirits. When performing solo, your "others" are invisible. We are all attended by lifelong spiritual guides. As well, the Spirit can assign spiritual guidance to assist us with specific tasks or concerns. When concentrated on yourself or when alone, step two recognizes the fact of being attended and assisted by angels and other supportive spirits.

Personally, I perform Spirit-to-Spirit every morning to establish an open heart for the day. I also use it when requiring a spiritual "booster shot" as the day goes on, and then again at night to relax. I use it to ask for omens and signs to aid in decision making. It also helps me meditate and pray, seek spiritual guidance, open to healing energies, set a manifesting intention, recover after a disturbing event, and more. Spirit-to-Spirit is your direct connection to the Spirit for any need.

As I walk you through this exercise, I'll help you attune to the various forms of intuition within each step. And after you run through this version of Spirit-to-Spirit, you'll be shown a few ways to apply it.

PREPARATION/INTENTION: There is actually no preparation necessary to conduct Spirit-to-Spirit for only yourself, unless you want to set an intention, such as "I would like to know how to deal with this upcoming situation" or "I would like signs to help me make a decision." You can conduct Spirit-to-Spirit for yourself anytime, anywhere, and with no groundwork.

Step One: **Affirm Your Own Spirit.** Acknowledge the immortal self you are, have always been, and are becoming. If you are verbal, simply state something like this: "I uphold only my truest and highest nature." If you are visual, picture the energies that depict your spiritual essence.

Step Two: **Affirm Others' Spirits.** This step connects you to your spiritual guides. Ask to fully bond with the spirits that surround and support you. You might sense a supportive link with these beings or use a statement like this one: "I am fully supported by the beings of Spirit that attend me." Use your visual intuition to picture these beautiful beings and perceive their love and light streaming to you. If you are mystical, any or all of these intuitive faculties will come into play.

Step Three: **Affirm the Spirit.** Know that all is being made well through the power and grace of the Spirit. Drop into the comfort of being loved and protected. If you asked the Spirit to assist you with an intention, trust that the Spirit will do this, and remain open to guidance and assistance.

Additional Insights and Scenarios

PERSONAL FOCUS

There are thousands of reasons to perform a basic Spirit-to-Spirit for just yourself, with no goal in mind. Most of the individuals I've taught this process to inform me they receive the following benefits:

- Improved mood

- Resilience under stress

- Ability to establish instant or better boundaries if needed, especially if trapped in an unexpected situation

- Knowledge of when to talk or act—or not

- Improved performance

Because of these benefits, I recommend performing the simple Spirit-to-Spirit exercise with your guides once or twice a day and at night, leaving the results open-ended.

Following are a few additional ways you can employ Spirit-to-Spirit for yourself.

Opening to Signs and Omens

Once in a while we could all use a nudge in the right direction. Using Spirit-to-Spirit to ask for signs is an ideal way to receive guidance and input.

Signs are revelations or sightings that deliver a message or advice. They can originate in the natural environment or within a psychic space. For instance, you might want to know if you should sell your house or not. The Spirit might respond by having you overhear a conversation at a coffee shop in which someone is telling their friend that they should move. Or perhaps three real estate flyers are delivered in your mailbox that day. These are indications received environmentally.

Psychically, a deceased ancestor might appear in a dream, show you a map, and point to a geographic area. Perhaps a voice speaks and tells you what to do. Whatever occurs, Spirit-to-Spirit can be instrumental in opening to signs.

If you are interested in employing Spirit-to-Spirit for receiving direction, I recommend that you establish a set amount of time in which to obtain insight—such as three days, a week, or a month—and then pay attention to extraordinary events during that time frame.

As an example of the effectiveness of this process, I worked with a man who couldn't decide if he should remain in a stressful marriage or not. I suggested that he use Spirit-to-Spirit to gain insight before our next appointment. He returned two weeks later with a well-scribbled journal. (Previously, he'd never kept a journal.) There were dozens of insights he felt he'd received from the Spirit in his waking and dream time. In the end my client left his marriage, but he did so in an upstanding way.

You can establish an intention for receiving a sign with a focus like this: "Within two weeks I will receive and recognize a sign to help me make a decision" or "I would like to know what to do about XYZ within a month."

When Praying

Praying involves talking with God. You might want to be heard or share a need. You might want to request a specific action from the Spirit or even lodge a complaint. It's okay to be real; for instance, you might set an intention such as "Spirit, I want to tell you why I'm angry with you."

Know, too, that prayers have a way of evolving. You might ask the Spirit to send you a puppy and then be directed to volunteer at a local shelter. If you feel like praying about anything, use Spirit-to-Spirit and remain in the flow.

When Grieving

Loss is intertwined with life. Spirit-to-Spirit can carry us through a grieving process and right into the light at the end of the tunnel.

Usually we don't have to establish a goal when grieving. We can simply conduct Spirit-to-Spirit whenever we feel sad, despairing, angry, or just plain loss, and allow the Spirit to attend us. Sometimes we might need help with our grieving process. Maybe we're stuck in the past and can't get over a long-ago trauma. (If this is the case, you might also want to read through chapter 9, which is devoted to clearing and recovering from trauma.) Maybe our emotions are locked away or taking control. Why not ask for assistance from your invisible spiritual team, as well as from the Spirit? Statements such as the following can open the door for supportive interactions between yourself, your guides, and the Spirit.

- If grieving childhood wounds:
  "I would like help recovering from childhood abuse/trauma/neglect."

- If grieving a current loss:
  "I need assistance to cope with this loss."

- If the grief is stuck and never ends:
  "I would like support in bringing this grief to a transformative conclusion."

- If there is resistance to the grieving process:
  "I accept assistance in accepting the blessings of my loss."

Mourning involves several stages, including denial, anger, bargaining, depression (sadness), and acceptance. The Spirit will walk you through them all.

Summary

Spirit-to-Spirit is a fundamental process that can be used for all situations. It can be employed during interactions with others or for personal use, for a stated purpose or without a goal. Whether or not you engage Spirit-to-Spirit with an intention, the three steps are the same. You affirm your personal spirit, affirm others' spirits or your own spiritual helpers, and finally affirm the Spirit.

CHAPTER FOUR

Healing Streams of Grace

After developing Spirit-to-Spirit, I knew there was still a void in my medicine kit. How best to enable transformational change? Through research and experimentation, I developed the missing technique. It's called Healing Streams of Grace, and I'd like to introduce it to you through an example.

A couple of years ago I received an email from a former client, a successful attorney. I had worked with Jerry, as I'll call him, three times the previous year. He was a career success but a flop romantically. Basically, he kept meeting, dating, and marrying various versions of his mother, a verbally abusive narcissist.

Before we leave childhood, our chakras are programmed by our surroundings and our reactions to them, as well as other factors discussed in chapter 2, such as past lives and ancestry. Once we leave home, what we're exposed to becomes what we attract. In Jerry's case, this meant he was the cog that fit another's wheel—the wheel being a rendition of his mother.

In order to break his relationship pattern, Jerry had undergone years of therapy, including cognitive analysis, hypnosis, and emotional trauma release. But to date he'd enjoyed zero functional relationships.

During our first two sessions, Jerry and I mainly talked. In the third session, I began the session with Spirit-to-Spirit, which I always do, and then asked the Spirit to connect this man with the Healing Streams of Grace needed to clear his dysfunctional energetic patterns and bring in the relationship that the Spirit would desire for him. The process took two seconds. I didn't have to do anything; neither did my client. Both of us were willing to let the Spirit direct these streams of energy. Jerry was willing to turn the outcome over to the Spirit.

Within a month Jerry had met two different women. Both women were friendly, but one was shyer.

He decided to date Woman One, the most overtly friendly woman. However, his car wouldn't start before the first date, so it never happened. When he tried to reschedule, his phone wouldn't work. He got the message and took out Woman Two. Within a few months he found himself in "a relationship better than any I could have imagined."

The force creating this shift were the Healing Streams of Grace, rays of energy that emanate from the Spirit. Whereas Spirit-to-Spirit establishes the foundation for the highest outcome, energetic boundaries, and appropriate agendas, the Healing Streams of Grace are composed of active energies that stimulate actual change. Not everyone is granted a miracle, as was Jerry. Then again, Jerry had gone through years of emotional processing, which probably enabled a quicker response from the universe. Healing streams of grace don't allow us to bypass our emotions or life lessons, but they do promote a flow of powerful energy between ourselves or others and the Spirit, and because of that, almost anything can happen.

In this chapter I will first explain the Healing Streams of Grace, covering what they are, how I discovered them, and what you can accomplish by using them. In this discussion I'll differentiate between the two basic types of Healing Streams of Grace, which I'll also refer to as *healing streams*, *streams of grace*, and *streams*. These two types are universal and personal.

I'll then present two exercises. The first exercise showcases the universal streams, and the second technique incorporates the personal streams. After the first exercise I'll show several different ways to direct the streams, such as when performing healing and manifesting; releasing entities, cords, and curses; establishing energetic protection; charging a physical substance; interacting with the chakras; dealing with difficult people; and interacting with situations in which you feel powerless. The second exercise will reveal how to open to a personal stream of grace and enable a direct and unique bond to the Spirit.

I promise you, you'll love this technique. Quite simply, it will fill your world with grace.

What Are Healing Streams of Grace?

We know the world is full of smog, fog, and darkness. What is sometimes harder to perceive are the beautiful streams of light and love—or grace—that are available to everyone all the time.

My definition of grace is love empowered, or love that creates more love. We are on this planet to generate love. If we're born into circumstances less than loving, or worse, hateful, we are charged with learning how to transform the hatred into love. If we're in a relationship replete with love, the same is asked of us. The lovely flower that is our relationship is to be matured into an even more beautiful blossom.

Love isn't a simple thing. It doesn't come in one size, nor can it easily be defined, standardized, or compartmentalized. That's the magnificence of love. Because love is eternal and ineffable, it doesn't obey the rules of the darkness. It can survive and sometimes even thrive inside of cruelty and fear. Love is the flower in-between the cracks of a bombed-out sidewalk. It's the single mother who prevents her son from joining a gang. It's the hundred-dollar tip left to a waitress who needs exactly that sum to pay her college tuition.

After forming Spirit-to-Spirit, I sought an equivalent process to enable transformation and healing, even in the worst of situations. I wanted a process that could be used with all other techniques to empower them toward the highest outcome. My search included studying the famous great healers and spiritualists from across time whose results could only be called miraculous.

One of my main sources of inspiration was James Rogers Newton, MD, who healed thousands of individuals during the 1800s. His successes weren't attributed to his medical training but rather to his activities as a healer, or "miracle maker." He become so famous that he saw up to one hundred patients a day in a healing practice he opened in Ohio in 1858. Thousands testified to his miraculous healing prowess (World Research Foundation, "Dr. James Rogers Newton").

Newton's only technique was to gaze on his patients with love (Collins, "Extraordinary Healing Power of Love"). Believing that everyone is one through the Father, Newton described himself as a medium. He explained that the angels and the deceased were available at all times, ready to deliver the healing energies continually provided by God. Indeed, it was a Welsh patient who best described Newton's spiritual healing energy, spying threads of light between himself and Newton during a healing. (Newton 102, 113, 258).

That Welshman hasn't been the only person that has equated unconditional love with streams of light. Bruno Groening, a well-known healer who practiced during the mid 1900s, also believed in God and said that the Creator's universal energy was continually available. He called this energy a "healing current" or a "healing stream" (Kamp, "Bruno Groning—A Revolution in Medicine"). Yet another famous healer, Phineas Quimby, who lived in the early to mid 1800s, was known as the Father of New Thought. His basic assumptions were that the "real self" is made of spiritual matter. Diseases and problems are a product of false thinking, but the loving power of the

Creator can penetrate these illusions and create healing (Cornerstone Books, "Phineas Parkhurst Quimby").

I determined that these individuals and hundreds of other sources had made the same observation: there is a Creator that continually provides healing streams of energy formed from divine love. I added the word "grace" to the formula because of a comment made by a shaman.

I had watched a Peruvian shaman in the Amazon heal a woman of a pus-filled infection during a ceremony. He had danced and sung and waved a wooden wand around. Over the next couple of hours the wound stopped seeping and began to close. Later I asked the shaman what had actually caused the woman to heal.

"Grace," he said. "Just grace."

Years later I amazed a class by administering Healing Streams of Grace to a woman who had a staph infection near her eye. I asked Spirit to bend the light supporting the infection so only the transformative light of the Healing Streams of Grace would enter the area. The next day the woman returned to class with the bandage off. She showed us a picture of what her eye area had looked like before joining the class. It had been inflamed and full of pus. Within twenty-four hours, the skin had closed and was healthy.

"It's the power of grace," I explained to the class. "It's not me. These are healing streams available to us all."

How Do Healing Streams of Grace Work?

As near as I can tell, Healing Streams of Grace are composed of the essence of all good things in this world and every other, including the heavens. There are healing streams made of grass, stars, breath, and earth. There are others formed from the echoes of the angels' songs and still others crafted from beautiful poetry. No matter what ingredients combine within them, the Healing Streams of Grace are ultimately streams of divine consciousness that create loving outcomes.

The best way I can describe the streams is pictorially. Visualize the Spirit as a sun. Our individual spirits are sparks coming off the sun. The Healing Streams of Grace are rays continually emanating from this sun. There are two main types.

Universal Healing Streams of Grace, generated by the sun (the Spirit), are constantly replenished. These beam wherever needed. If a child skins his knee—and he knows to ask for help—the streams would surround the knee. They would cleanse, soothe, and stitch tissue, drying a few tears while they were at it. (And in the first exercise provided in this chapter, you'll learn how to support a child in wielding the healing streams!) Healing streams can be requested for another person or being as well. Maybe the injured child runs into the house, not even thinking to ask for the streams. Mom can request healing streams to be sent to the knee. Since the Spirit is essentially in charge of the streams, they will only be attached if the Spirit approves. If for some reason that child doesn't require them—or instead needs streams for another reason, such as his emotions—only what is right will occur.

If a need has never existed before, the Spirit will customize streams for the situation. For instance, many of us are now experiencing the detrimental effect of the electromagnetic pollution caused by technology. Most likely, this is the first time that humans have had to contend with this challenge. Why wouldn't the Spirit formulate new streams of grace, updating the medicine bag so we can adapt to (and maybe even benefit from) technological fallout? I'll provide a short adaptation of a basic Healing Streams of Grace exercise to deal with exactly this issue.

Succinctly, the universal streams operate in these ways:

- The numbers or types of streams required for a certain cause are automatically provided.

- If none currently exist for the desired purpose, the Spirit will formulate new streams.

- The needed streams will attach where and when needed, shift as change and healing occurs, and drop off when the job is done.

- Spiritual guides sometimes accompany the universal streams. Assigned by the Spirit, they will instruct you in what actions to take through means including your intuition, dreams, and even signs that appear in your everyday life.

- The timing of all interactions with the streams—for all parties involved—is decided by the Spirit.

As well, each of our spirits is connected to the Spirit through personal streams of grace. These tailored bonds guarantee the flow of love between a spirit and the Spirit. No one else is linked to our personal streams. Ultimately the personal streams assure that we are personally nourished and protected, enabling us to embody our true selves in everyday life. We are so loved that the Spirit provides for each of us in ways particular to our personalities.

Figure 3 gives you a visual of the universal and personal healing streams of grace.

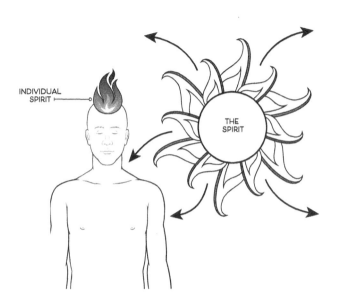

INDIVIDUAL SPIRIT

THE SPIRIT

FIGURE 3: *Universal and Personal Healing Streams of Grace*

There are two types of Healing Streams of Grace that you can request for yourself or others. Universal streams emanate directly from the Spirit and are available for anyone anytime. Personal streams comprise a direct bond between every spirit and the Spirit. These support the unique qualities of your own and others' spirits.

Many of you might wonder why we have to call upon the healing streams in order to access their power—or why, if they are composed of divine love, these streams aren't automatically applied to us or to a situation. One of the paradoxes of healing is that at some level, we have to call for and allow in the healing power of love. Consider the fact that the New Testament only features thirty-three healings conducted by Jesus. We have to presume that not everyone requesting a healing was healed or at least weren't altered in the way that they desired.

The truth is that we have free will. We have to deeply desire and give permission to be changed. Entrenched issues of unworthiness or unloveability can cause us to unconsciously block the healing streams. In fact, most of the famous healers I've studied suggest the same. We have to be willing to receive love for that love to enter and enable transformation. Because of this, the requested healing streams might first have to work in the subterranean depths of our psyche, preparing us for physical change.

The gift of free will can, at some level, also feel like a curse. We must ask in order to receive. But when we ask for transformation and really mean it, the healing streams can help us make gigantic strides.

An Example of a Universal Stream of Grace

I could share thousands of examples showcasing the properties and power of the healing streams. Sometimes their effects are magical and mysterious. The surgery works. The cancer heals. You find it easier to deal with a challenging person. Sometimes the streams simply shift reality so the right help comes to you.

As an example of the last statement, I was once at the dog park with my two dogs, Lucky the lab and Honey the golden retriever. Honey hurt his paw and lay down, whimpering. Lucky stood by, whining. At that moment the skies opened up and started raining. I had no idea what to do, and I was pretty miserable as I stood there trying to figure it out.

I always conduct Spirit-to-Spirit before asking for Healing Streams of Grace. In fact, I never employ the streams (nor use any other exercise) without first using Spirit-to-Spirit, for I want the Spirit and only the Spirit directing the streams. So I performed Spirit-to-Spirit and requested Healing Streams of Grace.

A woman jogged by and, despite the sleeting rain, stopped. She said she was an animal chiropractor. Could she help? As soon as she asked the question, the rain stopped.

She set Honey's paw, after which he could limp out of the park. When we got in the car, the rain started again. At home Honey continued hobbling but got consistently better. Within two days he was bounding around at the park again, catching balls and barking with delight. I gave the credit to the streams of grace.

How might you experience these streams? I'll share my experience next.

What Do Healing Streams of Grace Look, Feel, and Sound Like?

When I intuitively perceive Healing Streams of Grace, I feel like I'm in Wonderland. Every stream consists of multiple layers of color, sound, and shape. Some of the streams are thin and ethereal and others are thick and solid, like the trunk of a tree.

Some rise from the earth like ground fog and others blink into existence like sparks in the dark. There are long and short streams, vertical and horizontal, and others that form geometric shapes or rainbow hues.

On a visceral level I often react physically or emotionally to the streams when I'm accessing them for myself or others. The sensations are wide and varied. They can stimulate heat, warmth, freezing cold, or chill. They might cause tingling and itching or dancing and laughing. I might sense joy, fear, sadness, or despair. I hear the same reports from my clients. Sometimes a reaction occurs right away and other times, days later.

Once in a while the Healing Streams of Grace are delivered verbally. I once worked with a client who had experienced birth trauma as an infant. As soon as the streams entered, she started sobbing. She heard the "music of the angels," poetic lyrics assuring her that she was loved and wanted. My client's life changed dramatically. Because her self-esteem increased, her demeanor changed. She started dressing more boldly and displaying the creative side of her personality. Within a year she was offered a new job and was enjoying an amazing boyfriend. As she stated, "If the angels wanted me, although my mom didn't, I deserve to be happy."

Pay attention to your own experience of the Healing Streams of Grace. Take note and see if there are consistent patterns. If not, don't worry about it. There are more Healing Streams of Grace than could ever be counted.

A healing
--EXERCISE--

Healing Streams of Grace
THE UNIVERSAL STREAMS

The universal streams are always available, no matter the circumstances, predicament, or opportunity. The following steps are simple and clear. They represent all you must do to attract universal streams of grace for yourself or for others.

STEP ONE: **Perform Spirit-to-Spirit.** If you have an intention, establish it. You can frame an intention like this: "I would like Healing Streams of Grace to assist (myself/another) with achieving (insert outcome)." If you don't have an intention, don't worry about it. The Spirit will do whatever is needed regardless.

Now conduct Spirit-to-Spirit, first affirming your spirit and then others' spirits. Then affirm the Spirit, as taught in the previous chapter.

STEP TWO: **Ask for the Healing Streams of Grace.** Ask that the Spirit select the Healing Streams of Grace required for your request. Know that the Spirit will choose and customize the streams and connect them to you or to others. Then let go; allow the Spirit to take full charge. Request that you'll be provided additional instruction as needed, through omens, signs, or intuitive messages that you will easily recognize.

Step Three: **Gratitude.** Thank the Spirit for providing the healing streams—and trust the process.

Additional Insights and Scenarios

CUSTOMIZING THE UNIVERSAL HEALING STREAMS OF GRACE

It's extraordinarily easy to customize the healing streams for specific concerns. All you have to do is create specific intentions, remembering that the Spirit will shape the agenda and outcome to serve everyone and everything involved. To customize, simply create an intention before performing Spirit-to-Spirit.

Know, however, that you don't necessarily need to create an intention. It's enough to have or feel a need—

or cry "help" from your heart. The Spirit will hear the unheard and know what you don't know.

Following are typical scenarios you might experience and sample intentions. To explain these intentions, I first describe a common scenario, then share sample intentions, and, finally, provide an example.

Performing Healing

Whether you are administering a healing for yourself, another being, or a group, you can always use Healing Streams of Grace. It doesn't matter if the subject is present or not.

You can creatively come up with your own statement of intention or adjust the following request:

> *"I ask Spirit for healing streams to deal with the causes of (insert the problem)."*

Notice that I specifically request that the Spirit address the causes of the problem. Allopathic medicine tends to treat symptoms. Wholeness is achieved when we attend to the origins of a challenge, not only the surface appearance. The only healer that can assure optimum results is the Spirit. The Spirit will decide what truly makes us whole, which may or may not align with our opinion.

As an example, I used healing streams on a young girl who had been medically diagnosed with depression. Her father didn't like the fact that she was put on prescription medications. He brought her to my office, and we asked for streams of grace for his daughter.

He came to see me a few weeks later. His daughter was doing great, he reported, but he was upset with the outcome of the healing. Right after our session, the girl's pediatrician questioned the original diagnosis and referred the girl to a neuropsychologist, who administered a battery of tests and determined that, in fact, the girl had attention deficit/hyperactivity disorder (ADHD). After weaning the girl off the depression medications, the specialist put her on ADHD meds. As a consequence, the girl was prospering.

The father had thought the girl would be "cured" by the streams of grace and taken off all allopathic medications. Instead, she was correctly diagnosed and treated accordingly. Sometimes healing comes in ways we don't anticipate.

Opening to Manifesting

We all have dreams we'd like to manifest. Healing streams of grace assist in this endeavor by shifting the subtle energetic system, as well as our psychological programming and behavior. Consequently, we behave differently and also attract new situations. When seeking to help ourselves or another person, group, or being with manifesting, you can use a statement such as this:

> *"The Spirit now administers the Healing Streams of Grace needed to assist in manifesting (insert desire) in alignment with the highest needs of all concerned."*

Want to even more effectively supercharge your manifestation? Return to chapter 1 and examine the illustration on page 33 or the chakra chart beginning on page 34. Select the chakra related to your dream and create an intention like this:

> *"I affirm that the Spirit is sending Healing Streams of Grace to the (name of chakra) to enable me to manifest (insert the desire) in alignment with the highest needs of all involved."*

When it comes to manifesting, it's important to know that the Spirit will help manifest desires that benefit everyone concerned, not only a single person. Time and time again, I've watched several lives improve although only one person requested the streams. For example, I recently applied the healing streams to a teenage boy who was estranged from his father. Within a short amount of time, the boy felt empowered to discuss his frustrations with his father, who broke down emotionally and entered therapy.

Because of the counseling, the boy's father made peace with his own estranged father, who was a recovering alcoholic.

As another example, I once used Spirit-to-Spirit and then Healing Streams of Grace to manifest a new babysitter. I had one week to find a replacement for our current sitter, who was moving. I was sitting in a play area at a mall and another mother started talking. She shared the name of a daycare operator she had just met—a woman I had known when I was a child. Within another two hours, I had my new sitter. This sitter was in dire need of a replacement for a child who was leaving her care. She couldn't afford a gap in her income.

Releasing Attachments

When I was being trained in energy healing, I was told to "cut the cords," or sever the connections, between myself or others and dark influences. I introduced attachments in chapter 2, explaining how cords, curses, and other energy bindings forge unhealthy contracts between the living and negative entities, energies, familial ancestors, other living beings, demons, and the like.

Plain and simple, don't cut cords or simply hack away at an attachment. Chopped-off connections worsen matters and create additional problems. Mainly this is because the deeper issues or reasons for the bond haven't been addressed. As strange as it seems, the parties involved usually believe that these contractual agreements are meeting their needs. If the underlying issues aren't attended to and the cords are cut, the parties will attract similar mistreatment. Many times, the two original contract holders simply reconnect.

As a further explanation, picture a sawed-off electrical cord. Basically, it's a live wire, with charged energy sparking out the gaping end. These charges will continue to emit and attract matching frequencies. Pretty soon the cord will rebuild, either with the original person or being or a similar one.

True healing transforms the toxic energy bound in or flowing within an attachment so it doesn't attract similar negativity.

Healing streams of grace are the perfect solution for releasing attachments with mercy. The basic process is to ask Spirit to flow the streams inside and around the entire binding. The streams will neutralize the negative charges and also dissolve the "connection piece," such as the cord or miasm. As well, healing streams will assist the involved parties with working through their issues. The result is the safe disintegration of the attachment and an invitation for transformation in a timely manner—Spirit's timing, that is.

A sample intention, which can be used for self or another if releasing attachments, is as follows:

> *"I give permission for Spirit to dissolve*
> *the attachments causing harm in a way*
> *that enables true transformation and healing."*

I remember once working with a professor in Russia when I was teaching abroad. He had participated in a shamanic ceremony in the Ural Mountains. At his request, the shaman had cut a cord between the professor and his ex-wife. Since then, the professor's ex-wife had become completely erratic. She was showing up at his home and workplace only to scream and yell, insisting that they get back together.

I asked for Healing Streams of Grace to fill in and surround whatever remained of the cord or the stumps leftover from the shamanic work. My client immediately felt calmer. He wrote a few weeks later and said that he and his ex-wife had a "normal conversation" not long after the healing. They had cried together and then wished each other the best. Since then, my client wrote, they hadn't had any contact.

Dealing with Entities and Negative People— Bubbles of Truth

For the most part, I help people release entities by using the previous exercise for releasing attachments. Sometimes releasing cords or curses isn't enough. Sometimes we need to interact with the entity, negative influence, dark force, or hidden aspect of a problematic person in order to find out the reason that there is a connection.

In order to accomplish this goal, I ask the Spirit to form a "bubble of truth" by surrounding the entity with Healing Streams of Grace. Sometimes we're dealing with a living person and believe an aspect of them is harming us. In this case, follow the same procedure and ask the Spirit to encompass the negative aspect of this person with Healing Streams of Grace. An entity or harmful source has to be truthful while cocooned inside this bubble, which is entirely composed of the streams.

At this point, I'll ask questions of the interference. Ultimately, a victim wants understanding of the following from the interference:

- Why are we connected?
- What do you gain from the bond?
- What have I been gaining from the connection?

- What energies are we exchanging?
- What do you really look like?
- What issues are you avoiding through this bond?
- What are you allowing me to avoid through this connection?
- Are you willing to be released to the Spirit?

Know that it doesn't matter if an interfering entity or being is willing to be released from the bond. A victim always has the right to freedom; they just don't know it. It becomes easier to surrender the interference to the Spirit, releasing one's self from bondage, if you first figure out what wisdom can be culled from the interaction.

For example, years ago I worked with a psychiatrist who had struggled with insomnia since she was a child and believed that an entity was disturbing her at night. During a session I asked the Spirit to surround the entity with Healing Streams of Grace and to form a bubble of truth.

My client visualized this bubble, which makes all things appear as they really are. Within it appeared a small boy. The spirit boy and my client conversed. It seemed that this being was a "disappearing twin" and that my client's mother had been pregnant with two children, but only my client had survived the pregnancy. (Up to 30 percent of all pregnancies might involve a twin that "vanishes" in the first trimester [Twin Preganancies and Beyond, "Vanishing Twin Syndrome."]) The small boy was the soul that had been linked to the miscarried embryo. He hadn't wanted to leave and had kept trying to engage with his sister.

Through the communication my client was able to forgive this soul for its intrusiveness. She also gained insight into the nature of love and learned that not everything that seems bad is actually bad. We asked the Spirit to take the soul to the other side so he could be fully loved and helped. The spirit boy left with a smile, carried on the wings of angels.

This example showcases one of the many benefits of creating a bubble of truth. Not only do Healing Streams of Grace reveal the entity or energy causing a disturbance, but it allows a conversation between beings, if needed. In this way, the bubble serves as a sort of "suitcase" in which the Spirit can transform the entity or remove it safely.

There are other uses for the streams as a bubble of truth. If I'm feeling unsafe because of darker or confusing influences, whether the beings involved are alive or not, I can insert myself in a bubble of truth. In this way, I can't be manipulated, I can't manipulate, and I'll be safe.

For instance, perhaps I'm not speaking my truth with my boss, who is abusive. Encompassed in a bubble of truth, however, I'll feel more secure and able to communicate from a more honest place.

As well, I sometimes ask the Spirit to enfold someone else in a bubble of truth if it seems best for them. Imagine that you are concerned about a minor or an elderly person, and you aren't in a position to help them. You can ask the Spirit to surround the other person in a bubble of truth for their own well-being. I did this once for the neighbor of a client of mine. The neighbor was an older woman. My client was sure she was being taken advantage of by her children. Within a few weeks another relative uncovered financial abuse and called the authorities.

I also suggest employing bubbles of truth if your own or another's loved ones are being intimidated. A common ploy on the part of negative people and entities is that they coerce the living by threatening to injure a victim's loved ones. A real-life example is the abusive husband or wife who tells their spouse that if they get a divorce, they'll kidnap or injure the children. Entities also use this bully tactic.

How do you deal with this situation? Ask the Spirit to surround everyone and everything concerned with Healing Streams of Grace in the form of the bubbles of truth, which also serve as energetic protection. (Also see the next section, "Establishing Energetic Protection.")

Intention statements for forming bubbles of truth are quite simple:

> *"I ask the Spirit to fully surround _____ in Healing Streams of Grace formed as a bubble of truth."*

Establishing Energetic Protection

You can always ask the Spirit to provide a bubble of truth for yourself or another if protection is needed, as you were shown how to do in the last section. I use the bubbles if the situation is deadly or severe. If the circumstances are merely annoying or troublesome, I simply ask the Spirit to encompass myself or another in the Healing Streams of Grace needed for energetic protection. An easy intention statement is this:

> *"Please, Spirit, provide _____ with protective Healing Streams of Grace."*

I constantly draw upon protective streams of grace for a multitude of reasons. When visiting an ill friend in a hospital, for example, I might surround myself with the streams so I don't pick up an infection. If a client is undergoing surgery, I request streams for them and the surgical staff so everything goes well. You'll find thousands of applications for drawing upon the healing streams to establish boundaries and protection.

Charging a Physical Substance or Object

Healing streams of grace are fantastic "booster shots" for bolstering the positive effects of physical substances and decreasing any negative effects. Frequently I ask the Spirit to send streams into or through substances or objects for a number of reasons.

For instance, if a client is undergoing chemotherapy, I ask the Spirit to run healing streams through the medicine. This accomplishes two goals. The streams boost the beneficial effects of the medicine and limit the side effects. If a client is allergic to nearly every type of food—and believe me, I've seen this—I suggest that they bless their food with the streams before eating it, reducing the aftereffects.

Many of my clients sense the energy in objects. This can sometimes interfere with their enjoyment of a precious item. The streams can cleanse the disturbing energies from an object or substance and enrich the life-enhancing energies. You can even bless paperwork, such as when you are filing a report or mailing in your tax forms.

Formulating intention statements for objects and substances is simple. This is a sample:

"I request that the Spirit bless this object/substance/
liquid with Healing Streams of Grace."

Interacting with the Chakras

Chakras, which were introduced in chapter 1, are especially influenced by Healing Streams of Grace, as both are key players in the subtle world. There are two wheels, or components, to each chakra, and the inner wheel, in particular, is immediately responsive to these streams.

The outer wheel reflects our survival issues and programs. It is encoded by factors from our ancestry, genetics, family of origin, childhood, past lives, and culture. Most therapies or healing endeavors address the outer wheels. Change is slow on these wheels, for there are layers upon layers of wounds and dysfunctional beliefs. These wheels do, however, reflect the cause or nature of a problem or concern.

Rather than use the streams only on an outer wheel, I instead focus them on an internal chakra wheel. The inside wheel, which looks like a void or a vacuum full of light and love, reflects our spirit. This aspect of the chakra has a direct connection to others' spirits and the Spirit. By sending Healing Streams of Grace through a chakra's inner wheel, only the highest energies will influence the chakra. See figure 4 to better understand the structure of a chakra.

As an example, I recently had a sore lower back. I'd been spring cleaning and overdid it. The lower back relates to the second chakra, as relayed in chapter 1. After conducting Spirit-to-Spirit, I requested that the Spirit pour streams of grace through the inside of the second chakra and, from there, distribute them wherever needed. My back immediately felt better, and within a day or so I had returned to normal.

To request streams of grace to be shared through the inside of a particular chakra or multiple chakras, you can use a statement like this:

> *"Spirit, please send Healing Streams of Grace into me through the inside wheel of _____ chakra/s."*

Dealing with Difficult People

There are certain people who are just plain hard to be around. Spiritually, we are tasked to refrain from judging them. As most experts state, the problem isn't the other person, it's our reaction to them. Having said that, I know full well that some individuals are highly toxic, period.

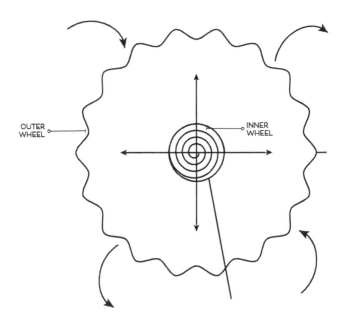

FIGURE 4: *The Inner and*
Outer Wheels of a Chakra

Every chakra has two wheels. The outer wheel exchanges
energy outside of itself and also receives energy from the
inner wheel. The inner wheel shares energy from its center and is the ideal place through which to flow Healing
Streams of Grace.

Using Healing Streams of Grace is not a tool for controlling or changing another person. We do have permission, however, to ask for Healing Streams of Grace for the person. Their personal spirit will decide how or if the streams will effect change. Know, however, that simply surrounding that always-complaining friend doesn't mean she's going to start being happy.

Whether or not you request streams for the problematic person, it's always worthwhile to connect yourself with healing streams when dealing with them. Saturated in this goodness, you'll be protected and also better able to make wise decisions. You might decide to stop seeing the cruel friend. You might become invulnerable to their criticism. You might find yourself speaking your mind or ignoring them. Whatever you do—or not—it will be guided by the Spirit and be perfect for you and all concerned.

If you want to use Healing Streams of Grace to support yourself with a challenging person, you can try these two statements:

> *"Please, Spirit, send Healing Streams of Grace to*
> *_____ to support their highest self."*

> *"I ask the Spirit to send and hold me within*
> *Healing Streams of Grace in regard to this person."*

When You Feel Powerless

In situations in which you are truly powerless, sometimes the only solution is to employ the Spirit-to-Spirit and the Healing Streams of Grace techniques.

We've all experienced these kinds of helpless moments where you're at the mall or a grocery store and you sense that a woman near you is being battered at home. Or perhaps you watch a couple interact, and it seems that one is an abuser and the other a victim. Or maybe you spy a kid walking in the street and you simply know he's being mistreated.

In these situations, you can't call the police or alert the authorities, as your intuition is your main proof of the problem. But you can request Healing Streams of Grace.

Most of the time you aren't going to know if your intercession was useful. But every so often, you'll discover that the healing streams have provided assistance. I was once stopped near a store by a homeless mother. She had two small children. I gave her a twenty-dollar bill but also wished Healing Streams of Grace upon the little family. About six months later, a woman came up to me in a store near that area. She pulled me aside and thanked me for the money. She said she used the money to feed her children but also take a bus to a shelter. That particular shelter helped homeless women get on their feet. She now lived in subsidized housing, had free daycare, and was working a job. I was all smiles!

Limiting the Effects of Pollution

These days there are endless sources of pollution. There are poisons in the air, water, and earth. Chemicals off-gas from our clothing and furniture. And between our electrical devices, cell phones, and power lines, among other sources of electromagnetic activity and errant sounds, we're constantly barraged by punishing energies that can undermine our physical, if not also psychological, health.

Every morning I thread healing streams throughout my auric field, requesting pollution protection. I introduced the auric field, as well as the variety of its layers, in chapter 1. Filling this field with Healing Streams of Grace helps prevent the toxic subtle and physical energies from bleeding into your body and chakras. To accomplish this goal, you can use an intention like this:

> *"The Spirit is now flooding my auric field with all the energies needed to remain healthy and toxic-free."*

If you are concerned about a known venomous source of pollution, such as your cell phone, you can focus the healing streams on the chakra and related auric layer that is most vulnerable. For instance, we listen to cell phones through our ears, which relate to the fifth chakra and auric layer. Ask the Spirit to flood this chakra and field with the streams of grace that will buffer you from the cell phone's side effects. You can implement an intention like this:

> *"I affirm that the Spirit is filling my _____ chakra and field with all the protection they need to keep me healthy and free of toxicity."*

As you might guess, the universal streams can be applied to accomplish so many more goals than the ones I've covered. There is a special set of streams, however, that can benefit you and you alone, which I will now describe.

Background on Personal Healing Streams of Grace

Universal Healing Streams of Grace are available for anybody and anything anytime, but there are streams distinct to each individual. In other words, there are personal streams unique to me, you, and all others—including my dogs, Honey and Lucky.

Our spirit is a spark from *the* Spirit. It is knowingly and continually connected to the Spirit and has been since time began. Guess what bonds your spirit with the Spirit? That's right: personal Healing Streams of Grace. These are especially created, fashioned, and sculpted by the Spirit for each spirit.

These personal streams are designed to bolster our spirit and also assist the embodiment of our spirit within our soul, mind, and body. When fully flowing inside and around us, we are completely aligned with the Spirit and experience enlightenment, or the state of wholeness. While these personal streams are always available, most of us have turned off the valves or at least hampered their free flow. Maybe we grew up in a family that didn't accept our unique selves. Perhaps we're still receiving the message that it's not okay to be ourselves. No matter the reasons, you deserve to have an active flow of grace between yourself and the Spirit.

Sometimes another person or being is preventing us from receiving a personal stream. Several years ago I worked with a client whose father was dead. Jerry, as I'll call him, could still sense the presence of his father—and his father's anger. Apparently Jerry's father had never wanted him to be an artist; rather, Jerry was supposed to have become a doctor, like his father. Even beyond the grave, Jerry's father seemed angry. It seemed like the father's disapproval was still blocking Jerry.

After conducting Spirit-to-Spirit, we asked the Spirit to activate one of Jerry's unique streams of grace. Immediately Jerry felt a bolt of energy throughout his body and a rush of forgiveness for his father. Over the next few months Jerry's art began to sell wide and far. Both of us suspected that his father had been given his own healing through the process and was more at peace.

I've discovered that many people have shut off (or have had others turn off) nearly all of their personal streams of grace. Others have cobbled together quite the plumbing system, allowing support into certain aspects of their lives and not into others.

The benefit of turning on a personal healing stream of grace—and asking Spirit to straighten out all the personal streams—is unexplainable. Each reverberates with a virtue or quality necessary to support all aspects of life. Each provides instant access to divine guidance, assistance, and an angelic team of helpers. Because they are so powerful, however, I usually activate only one at a time for myself or others. The next exercise will show you how to do this.

Healing Streams of Grace

PERSONAL STREAMS

Do you want to activate a personal stream for yourself or someone else? It's easy! Simply conduct Spirit-to-Spirit, first affirming your own spirit and then others' spirits. Then acknowledge the full presence of the Spirit.

At this point, simply ask the Spirit to activate a personal stream for you. (If you're working on someone else, you make the request for them.) Request also that the personal stream fully align with your body, mind, and soul and that it integrate within your everyday life. Know that the stream might assimilate slowly or quickly, but that you'll be safe throughout the process.

Finally, thank the Spirit for the gifting of this personal stream.

Universal or Personal?

Many people ask me, "How do I know if I should use a universal or a personal healing stream?"

You can use either. I turn to the personal streams for the following:

- If an issue has been chronic or caused long-term problems.

- If the person (or yourself) is undergoing a lot of change and transition.

- If they (or you) shares something like, "I've been missing something my entire life."

The main reason I limit the number of personal streams being turned on is that they are quite powerful and can take a while to integrate.

The universal streams, on the other hand, are available for anyone and everything, no matter what.

Special Instructional

TEACHING HEALING STREAMS OF GRACE TO CHILDREN

You can teach children how to ask for Healing Streams of Grace themselves.

First, I recommend shortening the phrase "Healing Streams of Grace." It's simply too long and cumbersome for most kids. Instead I use labels like "streams" or "light." Then I draw an image of these streams as beams coming off the sun and explain that they are always ready to be used to help or heal them. If a child is open to the concept of angels, I might say that this light is brought to them by angels. You can also select a different helper, depending on the child's spiritual beliefs, such as Christ or Allah.

I then tell the child that no matter what is going on, they can ask their angels—or God, the universe, etc.—to bring them the light or streams they need to deal with a personal need. I usually invite a child to practice with the streams before setting them loose with this practice.

There are a few reasons to practice with a child before leaving them to use the streams of grace on their own. Mainly I want to help them figure out how they'll know the streams are working. Like adults, children mainly operate physically, emotionally, visually, or verbally. They might also just "know" what is true, which involves the spiritual empathy process. I tell them that these are the ways that they "know things," preferring that phrase to going into the definition of intuition. Then I'll have a child select a need and ask if they can feel or sense the stream, hear what it sounds like, or see its coloration or shape. Now they are ready to ask their invisible helpers for a stream anytime they need one.

If the child can't sense the presence of an invisible helper, you can have them picture a figure from a well-loved spiritual book or source, such as one of an angel, Christ, Buddha, or Hindu god. You can also "enchant" a rock, asking that the Spirit connect it to an invisible helper. The child then knows that their helper "hears" them every time they touch the rock. And you can simply give permission for the child to "act as if" by suggesting that simply believing in the connection gives permission for the helper to reveal themselves over time.

I don't worry about not teaching youngsters to perform Spirit-to-Spirit before calling the healing streams; too many steps can be befuddling. Neither do I worry about whether they request a universal or personal stream. I believe that the Spirit will provide whatever is needed.

The other idea I like to teach children is that they can request a stream or light for someone else. Children can become worried when others are upset. Having an angry or scared parent can rock their world. Seeing others unhappy can make them unhappy. As well, most children I've worked with have a tendency to absorb others' energies. It's far healthier to send streams to others than to take on the other's negativity or worries. However, I always tell the child that God/Allah/the angels deliver the streams; the child doesn't need to do anything. Also, the helpers will figure out how to best help the other person. It's not up to the child.

* * * * * * *

Summary

Healing streams of grace are emanations of the Spirit available for improving all situations. You call them by setting a goal and conducting Spirit-to-Spirit. The Spirit now delivers the needed streams, of which there are two basic types. Universal streams can be requested for any situation and any type of being. They will remain attached until they are not needed anymore and will automatically transform as a situation progresses. Personal streams link the Spirit directly with an individual spirit and support the unique qualities of that being.

* * * *

CHAPTER FIVE

Transformation Through the Elements

Elements have been part of Eastern and indigenous healing modalities for thousands of years. For example, traditional Chinese medicine (TCM) proposes five elements that are aspects of *chi*, or life energy. Everything in the world is composed of these elements, each of which reflects specific characteristics and traits. Every element is also related to an identifiable emotion, season, subtle energy channel, and set of effects.

Tibetan medicine also advocates a five-element system, although the list differs slightly from the TCM account. The North American Lakota tribe embraces four elements, as did the ancient Mayans. Many of the North and South American tribes relate elements to directions, as well as specific animals and higher beings.

The ancient Celts believed that plants, trees, stones, and stars are formed by elements but that entities are in charge of these elements. For instance, certain devas, or fairy beings, manage the elements associated with tulips. Another grouping might oversee oak trees. The link between elements and beings isn't exclusive to this culture. Cultures ranging from the ancient Babylonians to African tribes frequently personified the gods as elements or linked spirits to elements.

No matter which continent we visit, the general takeaway is that the world is constructed from elemental, or natural, ingredients that determine the nature of a thing, person, situation, or action. As well, particular entities regulate these elements, assuring a safe and ethical use of the elemental powers.

In my own intuitive and healing practice, I work constantly with the elements. I use my knowledge of the elements—and, more specifically, the subtle elements—to assess the cause of issues, the state of psychological and energetic boundaries, the nature of someone's personality, and the underlying reasons for mental and emotional distress. I also employ my experience with the elements to assist with healing and to support manifesting. Overall, I have determined that the elements affect nearly every life issue physically, psychologically, and spiritually. Having studied elements in countries around the world, I have developed my own expanded list and description of eleven elements.

In this chapter I familiarize you with these eleven elements and explore what each can accomplish. I then share four exercises designed to help you apply elemental knowledge. These exercises, in order of appearance, will relate elements to grounding and protection, healing, and manifesting. The last exercise will show you how to link with elemental beings. As well, the first exercise, Grounding and Protecting with the Elements, can be used before or with Spirit-to-Spirit to help you anchor in your body and prepare for meditative or healing work.

But first, let's explore the three levels of knowledge required to make full use of elemental wisdom. This information will prepare you for the exercises, each of which will start with Spirit-to-Spirit, the technique featured in chapter 3. Many of the elemental exercises will also employ the Healing Streams of Grace discussed in chapter 4. No matter how frequently you decide to tap into the data in this chapter, either personally or professionally, know that the elements are always there for you and always part of you.

The Three Levels of Elemental Interactions

There are three lenses through which to view the elements. This knowledge will give you an understanding of the elements' beauty and complexity and help you apply elemental knowledge. These levels involve understanding the elements as physical energies, as subtle energies, and as related to elemental beings.

Elements as Physical

Each element is a physical component of the natural world. You can literally see, touch, smell, feel, or otherwise substantiate an element's existence. The elements that I work with are earth, wood, air, metal, fire, water, stone, light, sound, ether, and star (made of fire and ether).

This list includes all the elements I've learned about in my various studies around the world. In addition, I've added two elements exclusive to my research: light and sound. While most people wouldn't refer to light and sound as elemental properties, I believe that they are. Everything we perceive in physical reality is composed of electromagnetic radiation, which is light, and mechanical energy, which is sound. How can we analyze or rearrange physical matter unless we account for these two energies?

The most natural-sounding elements, including wood, fire, air, and metal, are featured on many cultural lists. Not as frequently noted is ether, which is called *akasha* in Sanskrit and considered the first element. It's also named *space* in Hindu and Tibetan cultures, amongst others, and is considered the essence of emptiness. Many of the ancients believed that ether births all the other elements.

Ether also appears on many Western depictions of the elements, especially amongst medieval scientists. At times Westerners have spelled it as *aether*, and it has sometimes been called quintessence. It's basically been considered the fifth element, or the element beyond all others. In general, the "normal" elements are measurable and ether is immeasurable. As it is commonly compared to heavenly energy or wisdom, I consider it equivalent to consciousness.

To my knowledge, I'm the only author specifying an element called star, which I define as a combination of fire and ether. Fire is the energy of power, passion, vitality, and ignition. Ether is consciousness. The star element is therefore "ignited consciousness," or consciousness that initiates transformation and change. I have included star energy in my work for almost twenty years, and hundreds of clients have benefited from its powers, especially people who believe that they are associated with other planetary or star systems.

I've met hundreds if not thousands of people who state that their souls once dwelled on other planets, only more recently incarnating on Earth. Still others have asserted that their earthly ancestors settled on Earth after traveling from the stars. I don't find these statements unbelievable at all. Dozens of cultures testify that their ancestors came from the stars, such as the Orion and Andromeda constellations, stars including Sirius, and planetary systems such as the Pleiades. One of the first times I studied with shamans in Peru, I dreamed about a past experience on the "Blue Planet." I related the dream, and the shamans nodded. They, too, had once lived there.

If a client was once linked to another planet or constellation, I use the star element to help them reconnect. Frequently their souls require a stream of this otherworldly energy to feel fulfilled and nourished. For instance, I had a client with several illnesses, all of which cleared up when he reconnected with his "home planet." He stated he'd been "longing for this energy" his entire life. He later reported that beings from this planet had started to assist him with his life, greatly improving his relationship and work success.

I present the particulars about each element in "The Specialties of the Elements" section later in this chapter.

Elements as Subtle Energies

As reassuring as it is to describe elements physically, I mainly work with them on a subtle basis.

In the Hindu tradition, the five elements are further subdivided into smaller and smaller parts. This concept occurs in other cultures, too. I believe this observation shows that all physical or obvious elements are composed of subtle elements, "mini versions" of the more material ingredients of the universe.

The reason this is important is that when conducting energy work, it's easier to work with subtle rather than physical elements. Of course, you could put your feet in water to draw more water into your lower chakras, but it would take forever to accomplish this task. It's far more effective to operate with the subtle elements. You can connect to them anywhere you are, even in a business meeting. You can breathe them in, wash your mind with them, and even imagine yourself patting them on your skin.

As silly as these examples sound, the truth is that if you aren't processing the physical elements correctly in your body, mind, or soul, it's because there is an imbalance in the subtle elements. I have found that when people balance their subtle elements, which can include adding additional elements or releasing those that are congested, the relationship with the physical elements shifts. In other words, I help clients recover from conditions or manifest their desires by first accessing the needed subtle elements and also releasing the congested subtle elements before worrying too much about what to do in "real life."

As an example, I find that many Americans suffer from adrenal fatigue and lack of nourishment. Our adrenals are part of the limbic system, which responds to stress by telling us to "flee, freeze, or fight." When we're overworked, our adrenals grow fatigued. We crave foods that comprise an "instant fix." You know what I mean: rolls, bread, candy bars, all the stuff that crashes our system further and causes candida, a yeast infection. Candida organisms are stealthy creatures. They steal our nutrients and thus deprive us of vital vitamins and minerals. As the candida is literally robbing us of our nutrition, we can now consider ourselves undernourished.

While a medical doctor or naturopath might tell you to eat better and drink more water, our system might be too far gone for these simple procedures to make a difference. I find that it's first necessary to restore the balance of the subtle elements. Once the subtle elements are balanced, our physical actions will make a difference. For instance, I might ask a client to visualize the flow of cleansing subtle water throughout their body. This will decrease the inflamed adrenals and also wash away the candida. I might have them pull more stone energy into their system. Stone is the basis of minerals. I will then gently increase the subtle fire in the adrenals over time, thus increasing the flow of life energy. Consistently I've found that if someone first affects change in the subtle elements, then the physical solutions can take root.

Sometimes I don't know exactly what I need to do to help myself or a client elementally. There is a shortcut for working with the elements by contacting the elementals.

The Existence of Elemental Beings

A plethora of invisible beings are linked to every element. You might call them devas, a name I introduced in the beginning of this chapter. I just use the term *elemental beings*.

In general, each grouping of the subtle (and physical) elements is associated with a group of entities. A fire elemental is an expert at fire. A water elemental can advise you about its specialty, and so on.

I use my intuition to relate to the elementals for many reasons. Sometimes I don't know which element I need to employ and so I contact the entire elemental kingdom. Usually, a spokesperson from the elemental group I need to work with emerges and tells me what to do. Sometimes I don't know how much of an element is needed or for how long. Elementals will inform you about how to use their associated elements and even administer the elements for healing and manifesting. These nature-based guides are a rich resource and can help with nearly any task, which is why I next want to instruct you about the specialties of the elements.

The Specialties of the Elements

Every element—and, therefore, elemental being—has well-defined specialties. Following is an outline of the elements and their major properties, including each element's protective abilities, healing aptitudes, and manifesting expertise. The elementals' descriptions are based on my own experience. I encourage you to develop your own relationship with the elements and their helpers. You will draw upon this information in the following exercises.

Earth Element

Major Properties: Foundation, comfort, and groundedness. Other qualities include responsibility, stability, consistency, firmness, stuckness, staidness, reliability, abundance, and the ability to build and buttress.

Elementals: Elementals are usually brown or another earthy tone and substantive, thick, and ponderous. They are often communally bonded, as if glued together.

Protective Abilities: Earth elements can erect a strong fortress around anything or anyone. They fill in empty spaces and decrease vulnerability.

Healing Aptitudes: These elements are perfect for knitting together tissue and acting as a bonding agent. They provide stability and fortification. You must unbind earth energies that are too stuck, at which point they create congestion and blockage. Examples of the latter include tumors and depressing emotions.

Manifestation Expertise: Earth elements are ideal for manifesting all material goods, including money, a home and its furnishings, career opportunities, food, and other material needs.

Wood Element

Major Properties: Rebirth, vision, purpose. Other qualities include cheer, buoyancy, friendship, power, strategy, truthful feelings, and potentiality.

Elementals: Wood elementals are usually earthy tones, green in particular. They take whatever shape they need to when supporting a change.

Protective Abilities: Wood elements will form rectangular shapes around the vulnerable and provide stability. They keep new plans on track until fully developed. Wood is a perfect element to insert into a child's auric field, as it will enable flexibility, joy, and maturation.

Healing Aptitudes: The subtle wood elements enhance whatever it is you are seeking to develop or strengthen. Wood can bolster and sustain everything from a teenager's emerging character to newly knitting skin. It guarantees flexibility and adaptability.

Manifestation Expertise: Wood elements ideally enable the beginning and initial growth of new projects. Call upon wood elements when starting anything new or seeking an innovative idea.

Air Element

Major Properties: Ideas, mentality, spread of data. Other qualities are freedom, trust, joy, clarity, lying, and honesty.

Elementals: Air elementals are often yellow, sky blue, or another light or pastel color. They are quick, pushy, and hard to see. They can also blink in and out of existence or quickly dart from one reality to another.

Protective Abilities: Like the wind, air elements can blow away everything from false ideas to negative entities, trap a harmful idea or being in a whirlwind, or create distractions.

Healing Aptitudes: Air elements can hold correct or dysfunctional beliefs; therefore, they can be used to transform inaccurate beliefs into helpful ones.

Manifestation Expertise: The power of positive belief can attract just about any type of opportunity or situation. Air elements can carry the knowledge, information, data, and instructions needed to accomplish a desire.

· · · · · · · · ·
Metal Element

Major Properties: Protection, transmission, self-worth, spirituality. Other qualities include boundaries, balance, self-worth, achievement, grief, insecurity, strength, resoluteness, focus, and righteousness.

Elementals: Metal elementals are usually silver, white, or gray. They are often geometrically shaped. When locked together, they look like a shape covered by a coating or sheen.

Protective Abilities: Subtle metal is protective of anything it surrounds, from an organ to an auric field. It deflects negativity and is receptive to truth.

Healing Aptitudes: As with wood, I use metals to surround all tender tissues, newly emerging personality traits, and protect new decisions or projects. But metal is even stronger than wood, as it can also keep out entities and negative energies and prevent someone from falling back into old or addictive behaviors. Metal can also form a boundary between people or a person and an entity. Heavy metal toxicity in the body frequently occurs in the areas that once needed and were

· · · · ·

denied protection. For instance, if you were physically abused by a father who beat you in the stomach, which is related to the third chakra, heavy or physical metals might line the organs in that area to promote protection. If you substitute subtle metal for the physical metal, the heavy metals and any clinging microbes, including virus, yeast, and bacteria, as well as related grief, can clear.

Manifestation Expertise: Ideal for manifesting situations that support self-worth and dignity and require a lot of perseverance.

Fire Element

Major Properties: Passion, power, and vivacity. Other qualities include enthusiasm, excitement, productivity, purging, anger, lust, anxiety, purification, destruction, happiness, and vigorousness.

Elementals: Usually small, quick, and "sparklike," fire elementals frequently form into columns, as if made of flame or smoke. They can be any flame color, although most are red.

Protective Abilities: Fire is scary. It is threatening. Fire energies destroy what is around them. If inserted in the auric field, fire will burn out microbes and scare away frightening people.

Healing Aptitudes: Fire purifies and purges, burning out microbes, toxins, dysfunctional beliefs, cords, and other attachments. Be careful, however, because fire can also inflame an already smoldering physical issue or emotion. Some inflammatory conditions exist because there is too much fire, others because there isn't enough. Determine the state of affairs in inflammatory areas before adding or reducing fire. (I usually do this by talking with a fire element, which you'll be shown how to do in this chapter.)

Manifestation Expertise: Fire will add additional fire to passions, bolstering a healthy or unhealthy desire.

· · · · · · · · ·

Water Element

Major Properties: Flow, creativity, emotions, and intuition. Other qualities include dreaming, sadness, despair, cleansing, adaptability, receptivity, family, flexibility, understanding, journeying, and humility.

Elementals: Water elements are usually mobile and flowing. They are often blue or black. When conjoined, they might form rivers of energy that can move through, around, and into any material and also travel between dimensions and realms.

Protective Abilities: The water element provides psychological and emotional safety and can repel intuitive information that isn't pertinent to one's higher spirit.

Healing Aptitudes: Subtle water specializes in healing psychological, emotional, and intuitive issues. Can cleanse, clear, wash, and replenish.

Manifestation Expertise: This element can attract intuitive messages and enable the manifestation of creative desires.

* * * * * * *
Stone Element

Major Properties: Fixation, storage of history, and preservation. Additional qualities include the ability to receive, contain, and send information across time.

Elementals: Stone elements take many forms. Stones range from river rock to gemstones, and the elementals look like the stones they are associated with.

Protective Abilities: The protective abilities of subtle stone elements differ according to the stone, but, in general, you can absorb the qualities of a particular stone and project them onto yourself or other.

Healing Aptitudes: These differ according to the stone. In general, stones carry the history of wherever they are from and provide data from the related ancient cultures, whether from this planet or another.

Manifestation Expertise: These differ according to the stone. In general, stones carry the history of wherever they are from and tell us how to manifest based on this data.

Light Element

Major Properties: Illumination, inspiration, sharing of love.

Elementals: Differ according to the type, source, and color of the light.

Protective Abilities: As above, but always creates what is most loving.

Healing Aptitudes: As above.

Manifestation Expertise: As above.

Sound Element

Major Properties: Empowerment and change.

Elementals: Look like sound waves or sonic ripples.

Protective Abilities: Differ according to type, source, and intensity. Always forces change.

Healing Aptitudes: As above.

Manifestation Expertise: As above.

Ether Element

Major Properties: Consciousness, wisdom, and transformation. Other qualities include timelessness, alchemy, magic, heavenliness, and divinity.

Elementals: Ether elementals can be transparent, white, black, silver, opaque, or shades of purple. They tend to be either foggy or crystalline in shape.

Protective Abilities: Ether is formless; the protection it provides is based on higher truths and wisdom.

Healing Aptitudes: If strongly administered and believed in, ether will bring the Spirit's will into all levels of a situation.

Manifestation Expertise: Same as above.

. . . .
Star Element

Major Properties: Ignition of consciousness. Burns away evil and forces illumination of higher truths and spiritual law. Links with interplanetary and celestial cultures to accomplish this.

Elementals: These differ according to type and source.

Protective Abilities: Star energy is a potent protector. It destroys lies and intensifies truths.

Healing Aptitudes: Star energy will literally get to the core of a problem, purge it, and show the truth that needs to be adopted.

Manifestation Expertise: This element will force the wish-maker to be clear about what they really want and then create a fire to manifest that desire.

Grounding and Protecting with the Elements

Accessing subtle elements is the key to being grounded, anchored in reality, and energetically protected. Basically, we need to draw the correct subtle elements into our body to be strong and safe.

This exercise can be done anytime you need a boost, feel depleted, or sense that you are endangered, either physically, psychologically, or spiritually. It also bolsters your immune system and supports your manifestation processes.

STEP ONE: **Spirit-to-Spirit.** Perform Spirit-to-Spirit by affirming your spirit, others' spirits, and the Spirit, and then relax completely. (Some people like to first conduct this entire exercise and then conduct Spirit-to-Spirit. I recommend you experiment with both processes.)

STEP TWO: **Focus On Your Feet.** Your feet link
to your tenth chakra, which lies underneath the
ground. Through the tenth chakra, you draw in
subtle elemental energies from nature. I believe
that these subtle elements then pass into the subtle energy system, which transmutes them into
physical elements.

The array of subtle elements required for
your own well-being differ than that required by
someone else. Because of this, you are now going to request access to the subtle elements personally required for your own highest interests.

To do this, concentrate on your feet and
ask that Healing Streams of Grace flow upward
through your tenth chakra and into your feet.
They carry the exact balance and amount of
elements that you require.

STEP THREE: **Fill Yourself.** Feel the subtle elements run up your legs and spine and then
into your head. The subtle elements spread in
every direction until they fill your chakras, your
body, and your auric field. As your auric field
becomes satiated with this replenishing and
protective energy, the subtle energies coat the

entirety of the field, creating an extra-strong boundary.

Step Four: **Accept.** Allow the subtle elements to completely nourish all aspects of your being. Know that you can tap into this stream of elements anytime you need, and that the Healing Streams of Grace will automatically update the types and flow of elements, so you are always receiving what you require.

Step Five: **Close.** Reaffirm your own spirit, the helping spirits, and the Spirit, then return to your everyday life when ready.

Healing with the Elements

This exercise is a powerful way to access the subtle elements to address a problem, whether it is physical, psychological, or spiritual. Use the descriptions of the elements provided in this chapter to select which elements you might need.

STEP ONE: **Conduct Spirit-to-Spirit.** Perform Spirit-to-Spirit with your healing goal in mind by affirming your own spirit and then others' spirits. Remain fixed in step three of Spirit-to-Spirit, surrendering to the Spirit's will.

You can also use the exercise on page 159, Grounding and Protecting with the Elements, to align yourself before or after conducting Spirit-to-Spirit.

STEP TWO: **Request Intuitive Insight.** Ask the Spirit to let you know what subtle elemental imbalances might be creating a problem or dysfunction. If applicable, request information about how these imbalances are affecting you.

Step Three: **Select Elements.** Which subtle elements need to be released—or added—in order to create a healthier state? Ask the Spirit to tell or show you why these elements are vital and important.

Step Four: **Enable Healing.** Allow the Spirit to shift the subtle elements to create wholeness and healthiness where there has been disease or imbalance. Know that Healing Streams of Grace are being used to assure the proper balance of elements and the ongoing adjustment of the energies. Accept the changes and ask if there is anything you must do to sustain or further the healing.

Step Five: **Close.** Thank the Spirit, all helping spirits, and your own spirit for the already-delivered and ongoing healing.

Manifesting with the Elements

Do you want to draw a fantastic opportunity into your life such as attract a better job, a romantic relationship, a sign or omen, or serendipitous joy? Achieving the correct adjustment of the elements allows you to set and hold an intention that can dynamite a dream into reality.

Know that by using Spirit-to-Spirit to create your intention statement, you affirm that the Spirit will support the dream in the best way possible. This means that you will only manifest what aligns with your personal spirit and also supports the well-being of all concerned. You might not get the exact particulars of your desire, but you will receive what is optimum. You might not be able to control the timing of the manifestation, but the timing will serve all concerned.

STEP ONE: **Perform Spirit-to-Spirit.** After conducting Spirit-to-Spirit by affirming your spirit, others' spirits, and the Spirit, you can also use the Grounding and Protecting with the Elements exercise on page 159 to completely align yourself at every level. Remain dedicated to connecting to the Spirit, the end point of step three in Spirit-to-Spirit.

STEP TWO: **Create an Intention Statement.** Intention statements affirm your desire. They also help your spirit adjust the subtle and therefore physical elements so you can attract situations, people, and opportunities to you.

To create your statement, formulate a single sentence that clarifies what you want, such as:

*"I am now reveling in my new job, which is
enabling me to use all my capabilities
to the fullest extent."*

*"I am enjoying the romantic relationship
I've always desired."*

*"I am now open to receiving signs to help me
make a decision about _____."*

Spend as much time as needed to create your
intention statement.

STEP THREE: **Set Your Intention.** Concentrate on
your heart. Breathe deeply and affirm the full
presence of the Spirit. Focus on your intention. Repeat it to yourself; you can even state it
aloud. Ask that Healing Streams of Grace infuse
your intention with whatever subtle elemental
energies are needed for manifestation.

Sense the healing streams flowing from your
heart and through your body, mind, and soul.
As they do so, they activate or bring in the subtle elements required to set the intention in your
body and energy system. Know that the Healing
Streams of Grace will continue to adjust these
elements.

STEP FOUR: **Close.** Feel gratitude for the Spirit and all spirits involved in making your dream come true.

Connecting with Elemental Beings

Elemental beings are great information sources. Most are eager to tell us how to use their related element and to provide ongoing insight. In order to connect with elemental beings, first perform Spirit-to-Spirit. Figure out which elemental community you need to communicate with and create the intention to do so.

You might intuitively sense, see, or hear the elemental beings associated with your selected element. Request that the community appoint a spokesperson with whom you can intuitively communicate. Ask that this spokesperson step forward. As you visualize or sense this being, inform it about your situation and ask for specific advice.

Make sure to request ongoing assistance from it and its community. When finished with this communiqué, thank the elemental and its group, as well as the Spirit. You can then continue with your life.

In the next chapter you'll be shown how to use Spirit-to-Spirit, Healing Streams of Grace, and the elements to effect easy change—and all with the flick of a finger.

• • • • • • •

Summary

There are eleven subtle elements, and each grouping is associated with subtle elemental beings. These elements are earth, wood, air, metal, fire, water, stone, light, sound, ether, and star. Every subtle element manages a specific set of needs and physical elements. If the subtle elements are imbalanced, you can experience physical, psychological, or spiritual imbalances. By employing Spirit-to-Spirit and Healing Streams of Grace with subtle element work, you better your chances of healing and manifesting.

CHAPTER SIX

The Light Wand

DIRECTING LIGHT
WITH A FINGER

The light wand is one of my favorite techniques, for two main reasons. First, it serves as an easy way to direct Healing Streams of Grace to help yourself and others. Through this technique, the healing streams direct light or another positive energy to perform a transformation. Second, the technique requires only one tool: a finger. Of course, you can also use multiple fingers, which you'll also be shown how to do in this chapter. Truly, this is a "be anywhere, do anything" technique.

After explaining the rationale for this technique, I'll show you multiple ways to apply it, but first I will show you how to differentiate between your receiving and sending hands. The first actual light wand exercise, called Aiming the Light Wand, presents the most basic version of the light wand. Through it you'll learn how to point your index finger and create change.

The next exercise, Elements with the Light Wand, encourages you to send elements via the healing streams to effect more precise change; elements were introduced in chapter 5. For your ease and convenience in employing the elements, I have included a section called Background Information: Elemental Magic with the Light Wand. This section describes the elements in terms of their main functions and can be used as a "cheat sheet" for selecting which elements to transfer through your light wand/finger. The final exercise, Fingers and Related Elements, is based on cross-cultural research and my own practice. In it I have linked specific fingers with specific elements. This information can help you pack even more punch in your light wand.

While manipulating energy through the light wand is a simple technique, it is one based on thousands of years of knowledge. By employing this technique you join the legion of practitioners who have known that there are actually few requirements for making change. At one level, all you need are your hands.

Understanding Healing Through the Hands and Fingers

For thousands of years healers in cultures around the world have directed healing energy with their hands. The simplest expression is a mother enveloping a child, making it "all better" with a hug. More complicated maneuvers include a physician performing surgery, an acupuncturist shifting chi (life energy) with the placement of needles, a conductor leading the orchestra with a stick, and a massage therapist releasing tension with specific moves.

Common sense suggests that the more controlled and directed we are with our hand or finger movements, the more precise the effects. For example, if I willy-nilly place a hand on a client's distended abdomen and ask for a shift, their stomach could potentially become even *more* bloated. When I want to create a certain outcome, I need to ask for it and direct the energy accordingly.

The light wand technique involves commanding energy toward a particular end using a finger or, in some cases, a set of fingers. You can always employ your index finger if you want to keep it simple. With that, the entire technique can involve pointing your index finger at a problem while decreeing a marching order.

For instance, if you want to clear an infection, conduct Spirit-to-Spirit, hold the finger near the poisoned flesh, and establish the intention of healing the infection. Healing streams of grace will be delivered to fulfill your request. If your goal is more elusive, you can point a finger at a chakra or a prop. For instance, imagine that you need money. The first chakra, discussed in chapter 1, manages money concerns. You can point a finger at your first chakra or write the word *money* on a piece of paper and point your finger, or light wand, at the paper, and *voilà!* The process of money making has begun!

For the process to be accomplished par excellence, you should select which hand to use or in what order you will use your hands. The reason it's important to assess for hand choice is that in terms of energy, we have a receiving and a sending hand.

In general, hands are an extension of the heart chakra. In order to keep our heart chakra balanced, one of our hands takes in energy from the external world and then deposits it into the heart center. The other hand moves energy out of the heart center and then sends it into the environment. If you want to get rid of problematic energy, you will employ a finger on your receiving hand, which will pull out that energy. If you want to add a beneficial energy into a situation, you will use your sending hand. In other words, think "receiving" as pulling/releasing and "sending" as pushing/adding.

Usually our dominant hand is our sending hand and our less-used hand is our receiving hand. I am right-handed and my sending hand is definitely my right hand. As expected, my left hand is my receiving hand. Typically, the reverse is true for a left-handed person. There are exceptions to the rule, however, which is why I provide an easy exercise for differentiating between your receiving and sending hands on page 176.

When I'm working on a client's tumor, for example, I want to discharge the energy causing the cancer and add energy for healthy cellular development. I use my receiving hand to release the cancerous energies and my sending hand to send in energy to bolster the body's immune system. At some point I might even employ both hands to accomplish both goals or to balance the effect of using each hand singularly. And I always utilize Spirit-to-Spirit before starting and then employ Healing Streams of Grace, which were introduced in chapters 3 and 4, when maneuvering energy. I usually ask that the healing streams flow around my fingers and around my hand so I don't take negative or unneeded energy into my system. The Spirit will dispatch all released energy and transform it for you.

You can use the light wand on nearly any issue. I once leveled my left index finger at my son's ankle. (This means I was taking energy out of the ankle.) My son had fallen and his ankle was inflamed and bruised. I demanded that any poisonous or toxic energy be removed, first using Spirit-to-Spirit in order to put the Spirit in charge of the process. I could feel the Healing Streams of Grace flow out of his ankle and around my finger before they dumped the pain and bacteria into the environment. There the Spirit disposed of it. Then I aimed my right index finger at the same area and asked the Spirit to emanate Healing Streams of Grace to bolster tissue healing. I felt powerful forces flow along my finger and enter the injury. My son's pain immediately abated, and within a couple of days there wasn't even any bruising.

I had a client use the light wand technique to send "tissue-softening healing streams" into scar tissue remaining from a long-ago car accident. She used the light wand several times a day for a few moments at a time. Within a month the scar tissue had faded to a point where I couldn't see it. I also had a student aim the light wand at her husband's first chakra, the energy center that manages manifesting and finances. He needed a job—quickly—so she used her sending index finger. Within a week he had secured a new position. He ran into a former employee at a coffee shop who offered him a job on the spot.

Another client used the light wand technique on her ill and aching grandmother who lived hundreds of miles away. She pointed her index finger at a picture of her grandmother and touched the areas where her grandmother was feeling pain or experiencing troubles. First she used her receiving index finger to pull out the troubling energies, and then she employed her sending index finger to share love. Her grandmother was on her feet within a week and said she had "never felt better."

All the shared examples relate to the simple version of the light wand, which uses a single finger. As stated in the introductory material in this chapter, you can create fancier practices by selecting different fingers and/or directing specific elements, as you'll be shown how to do in a bit.

And now, let's make magic.

Distinguishing Between Your Receiving and Sending Hands

Do you want to figure out the difference between your receiving hand and your sending hand? Start by shaking your hands and rubbing them together. Now hold them about two inches apart, palms facing each other. Sense the movement of energy between your palms.

You'll feel a flow of energy from one hand to another. The hand emanating energy is your sending hand and the hand accepting the energy is your receiving hand. You can retest your hands every once in a while if you think that your hands sometimes switch.

Aiming the Light Wand

The light wand technique is a powerful and easy way to bring about precise change. It involves selecting a hand and using your index finger to command transformation. Because a hand either receives or sends energy, you can then exchange hands, perform another command, and then use the index finger from both hands simultaneously to create balance.

This exercise will show you how to use both hands, although you don't have to. Through it you can focus on a bodily region, a chakra or auric layer, or create a prop. To accomplish this very easy exercise, you will start with the Spirit-to-Spirit (from chapter 3) and Healing Streams of Grace (from chapter 4) exercises. After you learn this basic exercise, I'll introduce you to exercises that will incorporate the elements and different fingers.

You choose the order in which to perform the two basic start-up activities. You can establish your intention and then perform Spirit-to-Spirit or do the reverse. Either way, the Spirit will shape the intention so it works best for you. Having said that, following are the steps to take to employ your light wand.

STEP ONE: **Perform Spirit-to-Spirit.** Affirm your own spirit, the spirits of all parties present and not present, and invoke the Spirit.

STEP TWO: **Set a Commanding Intention.** Decide what issue you'd like to address. Formulate it into an intention statement, which you will use to command change. Samples include: "I want to clear up this infection" or "I want to relieve _____'s depression."

STEP THREE: **Select a Hand.** Select your receiving or sending hand. You can ask the Spirit for guidance if you don't know which one to use.

STEP FOUR: **Aim the Light Wand.** Point your index finger, now transformed into a light wand, at the subject, bodily area, chakra, or prop. Command for the desired change, either aloud or inside yourself, asking that the Spirit's will be carried out. Ask the Spirit to deliver Healing Streams of Grace to implement your intention and hold your finger position until you perceive a shift physically, emotionally, or intuitively.

STEP FIVE: **Switch Hands (optional).** If you want to use the other hand, do so now, repeating step four.

STEP SIX: **Balance Hands (optional).** If you desire, aim the index finger from both hands toward the subject at the same time, asking the Spirit to balance the energies.

STEP SEVEN: **Close.** Take a few deep breaths and release the outcome of the exercise to the Spirit. Shake your hands and let your fingers transform from light wands to fingers again. Continue with your life when ready, first checking intuitively if you will need to repeat the light wand technique, and if so, how frequently and for how long. Thank your own spirit, the spirits of those involved, and the Spirit for the assistance.

A healing
—EXERCISE—

Elements with the Light Wand

Elements are so powerful that I frequently insert their subtle energies into my practice. As discussed in chapter 5, I work with eleven elements. If you are clear about which elements need to be released or administered, you can easily customize the light wand exercise to encourage elemental miracles.

After performing Spirit-to-Spirit, ask the Spirit to let the Healing Streams of Grace carry in or take out a particular element or multiple elements. For instance, imagine that you are dealing with exhaustion and fatigue. You might choose to perform the light wand exercise as presented in Aiming the Light Wand, but add the fire element into the Healing Streams of Grace. The fire energy will add vitality if you administer it through your sending finger. It will pull out inflammation if you conduct the light wand activity with your receiving finger.

Imagine that you need to make an important decision but you are confused. Why not perform an energy release using the element of air, which relates to ideas? Purge the dysfunctional beliefs creating confusion by using the index finger on your receiving hand, and then turn around and send air right back in to gain insight through the index finger on your sending hand. Or maybe you want to add water energy, which boosts your intuition and assures emotional clarity; it's up to you.

Should you desire this extra dynamic, refer to the following table to help you link the elements with the light wand.

Background Information

ELEMENTAL MAGIC WITH THE LIGHT WAND

Following is a rendering of the elements introduced in chapter 5. This "cheat sheet" covers the purpose of each element, as well as what you can expect to release and add when using the light wand.

element	purpose	energy released / receiving finger
Earth	Foundation	Stuckness/Excessiveness
Wood	Accomplishment	Indecisiveness/Weakness
Air	Ideas	Dysfunctional Perceptions
Metal	Protection	Grief/Clutching/Negativity
Fire	Passion	Inflammation/Toxins/Anxiety
Water	Flow	Fear/Interference
Stone	Stored Knowledge	Depression/History
Light	Love	Separation
Sound	Power	Manipulation
Star	Purification	Negativity/Lies/Evil
Ether	Consciousness	Untruths

energy added /
sending finger

Rootedness/Comfort

Growth/Determination

Creativity/Insight

Boundaries/Spirituality

Power/Vitality

Intuition/Emotional Clarity

Strength/Certainty

Connectivity

Highest Outcome

Directed Power

Wisdom

A healing
—EXERCISE—

Fingers and Related Elements

Cultures across time have associated specific fingers with certain elements. The ideas differ from place to place, so I have developed my own elemental roster based on research and experience.

If you feel drawn to supercharge your light wand, select a finger based on its associated element and use it to perform the Aiming the Light Wand exercise. You can also aim two or more fingers and pay attention to sending and receiving hands.

Following are my associations between the various fingers and the subtle elements.

finger	associated elements
Thumb	Earth and Stone
Index	Sound and Light
Middle	Fire, Ether, and Star
Ring	Air and Metal
Little	Water and Wood

Now that you've been apprised of many of the basic exercises I employ on a daily basis, it's time to move a bit more "off planet"—or at least learn how to travel near and far. The next chapter will prepare you to conduct the exercises that follow it. Featuring a safe and easy way to journey or intuitively roam across all times and spaces, chapter 7 will expand your repertoire exponentially.

* * * * * * *

Summary

The light wand technique employs a finger or multiple fingers to create change. After differentiating between your sending and receiving hands, you can direct change through your index fingers. More complex approaches allow you to select a finger or multiple fingers based on the elements associated with them. You can also enable transformation by sending elements through the index finger. This handy technique is a go-anywhere and do-anything way to enable mini miracles.

CHAPTER SEVEN

In-Body Journeying

Energy work frequently involves altering your focus so that you can "visit" another time and place. Destinations can include your own or another's past, a historical site, another planet, a concurrent reality, a possible future situation, and just about anywhere or "any-when" else.

The ancient term for time-space travel is *journeying.* Journeys are usually conducted by the soul or another subtle part of the self. A journey can be performed for hundreds of reasons, such as to uncover the source of a challenge, unlock secret powers, gather a healing energy, gain insight for a decision, or boost a manifestation.

In this chapter I'll explore the ins and outs of journeying, but even more importantly, I'll be emphasizing a specific point, which is this: *many of the contemporary versions of journeying are potentially dangerous or harmful.*

The perils of journeying lie in the fact that journeying traditionally involves projecting a part of the self outside of the body. As I'll explain in this chapter, this is a risky endeavor, yet journeying is a vital tool for transformation.

In order to eliminate the hazards, I've developed my own journeying technique, which I'll introduce you to in this chapter.

My journeying process is simple and elegant. It also allows you to remain in your body as you visit other places and spaces with virtually no limits. Ensconced in your body, you remain safe and protected, even though you're expanded and "abroad."

After learning more about journeying in general and the red flags involved in the standard processes, I'll walk you through a short journeying exercise. After practicing this technique, grab an energetic passport and away you go! You'll be employing versions of this journeying process through the remainder of this book.

What Is Journeying?

The medicine people of most cultures have conducted journeys across time and space and into different dimensions in order to assist the injured, hurting, or hopeful. They also have helped others perform their own excursions. How do these journeys differ from mental wanderings such as reminiscing about yesterday or planning tomorrow? These deliberate journeys have been traditionally conducted by a part of the self that leaves the body.

There are many parts of us that can conduct an out-of-body journey. These aspects include the soul or a part of the soul, but also another sub-aspect, such as an inner child, the mind, or our consciousness. We can also elicit the same experience in another.

Historically the soul has been the most frequent time traveler; hence, the most basic type of journeying is called the shamanic journey, soul flight, or soul journey. A more modern term for this travel is remote viewing. When remote viewing, a part of the self exits the body to visualize what's occurring somewhere else. Another term is astral travel, which is a journey that occurs on the astral plane, a multi-level dimensional meeting ground for beings from various realities. Another commonly used phrase is out-of-body travel or having an out-of-body experience, or OBE. The acronym OBE perfectly depicts the state of roaming beyond the physical body. And what are those lucid dreams, the nighttime experience of feeling awake even when asleep, but the product of a sleep-induced journey?

There are dozens of reasons to undertake a spiritual excursion. You might drop into your past to uncover the cause of an injury. Maybe you journey to the Netherlands to challenge a dark force or an alien invader or jet into the future to redirect it. Perhaps you want to chat with spiritual guides, visit the land of the dead, work through an emotional trauma, examine your own or another's health, or experience another way of being. As a tool, journeying is a vital way to create substantial results.

One of the reasons that out-of-body journeying works so well is that it involves freeing ourselves from the body's limitations. This is also one of the reasons that traditional journeying is so dangerous.

The Problem with Out-of-Body Journeying

A few years ago I stopped flying outside of my body or directing others to do the same. I was noticing the following side effects in the wake of a journey:

- Bodily endangerment during the excursion.
- Punctures or stretch marks in the auric field.
- Intrusion or implosion of others' energies.
- Threatening interactions with dark forces.
- Difficulties getting back into the body.

Why would an OBE create bodily discomfort or a wound? Think about it. The inner aspect of ourself that is journeying, which is usually a part of our soul but can also be a child-self or another part of our being, can't exit without projecting through the skin and auric field, thus pitting or breaking the field. If the journeying aspect doesn't return the same way, it can cause a new injury site.

When a part of us leaves, an empty space remains. A myriad of entities or energies can now leap in uninvited, including parts of other people or beings, dark forces, ghosts, or others' feelings, diseases, or desires.

Consider also the vulnerability of the escaped self. Unless it's energetically protected, it is exposed to whatever lies in the Great Beyond. I once had a client journey to a past life in which he had died from the bubonic plague. Although he worked through issues during the journey, upon returning he became violently ill for a number of days. He wasn't actually sick with the plague, but the subtle energy of the disease had reactivated in his soul and dumped into his body.

Remember that the wandering self is just that—a wanderer. Sometimes our nomadic self knows where it's going and how to get there; sometimes the path is more circuitous. It's not like we journey with a compass or a GPS. Even if we make it to our destination and return in one piece, the pilgrimage can be exhausting. It might feel as if we've barely survived a gauntlet or been lost in a labyrinth.

So what's a journeyer to do?

The key to connecting to any realm while remaining safe is to travel without leaving your body. This goal can be accomplished by journeying through your eighth chakra's bodily site, the thymus.

Your eighth chakra, which was introduced in chapter 1, is officially located about two inches above your head. If you enter the chakra's center, you'll find yourself in a central space. Hallways branch in every direction. Each can be entered with a door. These passages access every dimension, plane of existence, and time period. Of course, to journey through the over-the-head center is equivalent to exiting the body. The good news is that you can achieve all the benefits of the eighth chakra's interconnectedness by trekking inside the thymus. You see, the gateways to the universe are inside of you. The energetic arrangement of the thymus is identical to that of the above-the-head eighth chakra.

So if you want to experience safe travels, use the following exercise, which enables you to journey without even packing a suitcase. After all, there's no flight to catch. The journeying is conducted internally.

Inner Journeying

In this version of the journeying exercise, you will walk the universe via your thymus. During the process you will select a hallway to enter and employ whichever intuitive style you are most comfortable with. Above all, you will learn a process that can be conducted safely, no matter where you are heading.

STEP ONE: **Preparation.** Find a private space and make sure you won't be disturbed. Breathe deeply and focus on your thymus area. You can focus on a concern or a destination or simply let the Spirit figure out where to guide you.

STEP TWO: **Conduct Spirit-to-Spirit.** Conduct Spirit-to-Spirit, affirming your spirit, others' spirits, and the Spirit. While finalizing step three, which involves turning your will over to the Spirit, ask the Spirit to safely hold you inside of your thymus, the home of your eighth chakra. Now ask the Spirit to take you where you need to go and to accompany you on the journey.

STEP THREE: **Journey.** Request that the Spirit turn on the light around you. You'll find yourself on a white marble floor. It is iridescent and beautiful. You are surrounded by the blackness of outer space, which glistens with stars.

The flooring is actually a platform in the middle of millions upon millions of hallways, which stretch from the center place like spokes on a wheel. Each of these hallways is available through a doorway.

The Spirit indicates which doorway you should pass through and assures you that although you'll officially walk through the door, you'll remain within your thymus. The entire universe and all dimensions are available inside of this eighth chakra center. With the Spirit's assistance, you select a door, open it, and walk through. What you see, feel, sense, hear, or become aware of holds the answers to your query or shows you what you need to know. The Spirit will share teachings, reflections, and wisdom and then tell you when you are finished.

STEP FOUR: **Return.** Walking back through the door, return to the shining platform. The stars blink out and your thymus reconfigures into a "normal" organ. Slowly the Spirit returns you to the recognition of your physical, this-life state. You sense your thymus and entire upper chest and then reengage with the remainder of your body. Breathe deeply and become aware of your environment. Thank the Spirit, the helping spirits, and your own spirit for this journey, and return to your everyday life when ready.

* * * * * * *

Summary

Journeying is the art of visiting other times, places, and dimensions. It is best accomplished inside of the body rather than by puncturing the auric field when exiting the body. The simple practice outlined in this chapter allows you to journey inside of your thymus, the in-body site for your eighth chakra. You are now prepared for the many journeying experiences you'll conduct in the following chapters.

CHAPTER EIGHT

The Three Soul Records

The eighth chakra, the vehicle for journeying presented in the previous chapter, is rich in resources for the seeker of transformation. One of its most important roles is as a storage house and access point for three soul records, subtle energy libraries that possess distinct sets of knowledge.

In this chapter you'll learn about these three libraries and use the journeying technique taught in chapter 7 to travel into each. You can easily adapt the included journeying exercise to another person by reading it aloud and guiding them through each step.

You might already be familiar with the Akashic Records, the knowledge of which is rooted in ancient cultures and philosophies. The other two records, which I call the Shadow Records and the Book of Life, are unique to my work. Altogether, accessing these libraries enables you to gather information about all times and spaces, deal with regrets and resentments, and view situations as the Spirit might.

Your invitation into the mystical hallways of the soul will begin with an exploration of the three basic soul records. I then adapt the journeying exercise from the previous chapter to help you focus on a need while roving the pathways of each of the three records. In the end you'll discover that within the singular vehicle of your eighth chakra lies the story of the roads already taken and the adventures yet to come.

The Three Records of the Soul

As discussed in chapter 1, your soul is the part of you that travels across time and space. It incarnates within a physical body in order to learn about love.

My favorite image of the soul is as a beautiful ball of light beaming in infinite directions. Each of these arms touches into one of the many periods of local and non-local time, or concrete places and those that are yet to be manifested. The soul is a dreamer and a doer. It tows the past behind it, as does a water-skier, but also faces forward toward eternity. It lives in the here and now but also concurrent realities, a concept explained later in this chapter.

To track the myriad of details involved in time-space travel, the soul compartmentalizes its knowledge within three records. The information in these archives is collected in the body during a lifetime and uploaded into the soul at death. It is then downloaded from the soul's annals into a new body and specifically held within the eighth chakra, which is located above the head but also anchored within the thymus in the upper chest. While we're alive—and even in-between lives—the soul continues to data-stream and store newly acquired information within the records. Bottom line: anything and everything can be accessed through these three records.

Now grab your energetic library card—it's time to take a look at these three books!

The Akashic Records
PAST, PRESENT, AND FUTURE

The Akashic Records are a collection of mystical knowledge. The word *akashic* is Sanskrit for "space" or "ether." This means that, energetically, the Akashic Records are a storage of esoteric knowledge in a nonphysical place of existence. Cultures across time have perceived the existence of these records and worked with them for healing and manifesting purposes.

There are personal and collective Akashic Records. Your personal Akashic Records are found within your soul and bound to your eighth chakra. Contemporary practitioners describe these personal records as a series of subtle books, tablets, or scrolls warehoused in the soul's inner sanctum or energetic field. The collective Akashic Records are frequently depicted as a huge energetic library. The journeyer traverses the hallways of this library to find their own records but can also leap into another's library and check out their records. In this book, though, I'm going to familiarize you with how to access your own Akashic Records.

What might you discover when journeying into your records? Basically, you can uncover every actual or potential thought, feeling, event, situation, or action in relation to three time periods:

The Past

Everything you've experienced across time is immortalized in your Akashic Records. This includes actual lifetimes but also in-between lives. Also available is information about what past experiences you could have had if events had unfolded differently.

We journey accidentally into the past all the time. Think of how often you revisit a special moment or recall a long-ago conversation. In therapy we deliberately access our storyline to uncover and clear the dysfunctional beliefs associated with a negative situation. There is much more that you can accomplish in the past, however, if you understand the power of the Akashic realms.

For instance, through the Akashic realms, you can touch down at any this-life historical moments but also journey in-between lives or to past lives and even time periods occurring before the creation of the universe. You can shift perspectives and view a painful situation through another's eyes, boosting your ability to understand a cruel person and better separate from or forgive them.

You can also formulate an alternative past. By reimagining a different ending to a bad situation, you alter your subtle energies—and, therefore, your current reality. Imagine that you were killed by an abusive husband in a past life. By re-creating the event and surviving it, which involves constructing an alternative history, you could stop attracting this-life abusive romantic partners. Ultimately, perspective is king.

The Present

Through the Akashic realms you can observe what's currently happening in your life, but also perform numerous other empowering activities. You can perceive what's occurring within and around you but also envision the present through different lenses, maybe looking through the eyes of an enemy or friend. Again, perspective rules. By understanding a situation through diverse points of view, you can arrive at a truth that uplifts rather than hurts. You can also journey to another country or culture and check out what's happening there. Perhaps you're concerned about a loved one and want to find out if they need help. Why not visit them and check it out yourself?

There are even more esoteric tasks you can perform through the Akashic realms. Within these records are the *maybes*. Maybes are the realities you could be living if history had unfolded differently. Parenthetically, there is a Cyndi who could be married to someone named James and living in Europe—or maybe a Cyndi who might not be alive because she married Alfred, who killed them both through a drunk driving accident. While these "maybe" conjectures aren't technically real, knowing about them can teach us how to make better decisions or validate a decision we made. (I'm pretty happy I never met and married that Alfred guy!)

There are also different types of alternative or concurrent realities. These are realities that dwell "next to" or aside this reality. We might construct and live within an alternative reality for only a brief time or during the entirety of this lifetime. As an example of a short-term interlude, one of my concurrent realities was as a boy who, at age seventeen, died in a motorcycle accident. At that time in my "Cyndi life," I loved riding bikes. In the alternative reality I was killed by a car while riding a motorcycle. Once my boy self "died" and emerged from that alternative reality, my Cyndi self decided to stop riding motorcycles. Most likely, the short-lived experience as the boy saved me in my "Cyndi life."

Every so often I uncover situations that suggest a soul is experiencing their earth-life as secondary, while the majority of their soul abides somewhere else. For example, I recently worked with a client whose sister had lost a child who'd only lived about two weeks. My client was devastated, as was her family. The information that came through my client during our session suggested that the infant's soul was primarily living in another dimension.

There the soul was an older, stately man who exhibited no ability to love. An aspect of the older man's soul split off and became an infant in the earth world but passed away young because the mission was accomplished. As an earthly infant, the soul was unconditionally loved. The older man hadn't experienced unconditional love in the primary lifetime.

As a result, the older man's life completely changed after the infant soul returned to him, becoming softer and more giving and compassionate. The older man never really knew he'd been a "real" infant somewhere else. Rather, he experienced the infancy in a dream.

Reality is much more complex than we might think.

The Future

There are countless possible futures. The most solid potential future is a projection of the present. Every time we step forward, however, we close off certain roads and open up different ones, thus creating numerous branches or alleyways we could walk down. Then there are futures that form because of others' actions and futures that fork off the concurrent realities. As well, if you alter your perception of the past, you alter your current self. In reaction, new possible futures might spring up.

I constantly examine potential futures for my clients. My preference is to peer into the future for practical reasons. For example, a client once asked if she should take a new job or not. I guided her into the future that could possibly unfold if she took the position. She gasped in horror and asserted that she would be laid off almost immediately. She decided to remain in her current job. A few months later she discovered that the company that had wanted to hire her had gone out of business.

The Shadow Records

REGRETS AND RESENTMENTS

Think about how much suffering is caused by regret or resentment. Regret occurs when we wish we'd done or said something different. Resentment strikes when we wish the same of another.

Through my work I've determined that there are annals that contain these deeply guarded desires. These are the Shadow Records, and they function like an annex to the Akashic realms. Basically, all regrets or resentments are stored in this back room in the same manner that we shove overflow into a spare room or a catch-all kitchen drawer. We vow we'll sort through all the stuff, but we rarely get to it.

Psychically, I perceive the Shadow Records as a fog around the Akashic Records. This cloudiness is easiest to perceive around the eighth chakra or the thymus. You can also glimpse these billowing mists around the DNA, which hold our ancestors' regrets and resentments, as well as our own memories that spurred regrets and resentments.

Why would we journey into the shadows of regret and resentment? Plain and simple, regrets detract from joy and progress. When we believe that we should or could have been a different person in the past, we get stuck in self-recrimination. It's easy to become surly, shameful, or scared. We might avoid new opportunities and fail to achieve our potential.

The key to recovering from regret is to shift our perception so we can grab hold of the silver lining in the stormcloud. If we take the learning and leave behind the regret, any situation—no matter how difficult or embarrassing—can provide insight and inspire change. Once we own the teaching, we can release the subtle energetic charges keeping us stuck.

As an example, I once worked with a famous actor who was about fifty years old. He wanted to see if there was a reason he kept dating women in their mid to later twenties. "Not that I have a problem with it," he assured me, looking like a man of the world, "but my friends keep telling me I'm missing out on true intimacy."

I peered into his Shadow Records and saw an image of a woman with blond hair. She appeared to be in her mid-twenties. She wore glasses and beamed with a wide smile. Unable to obtain any other intuitive insights, I shared this one. My client blanched.

"That's Jessica," he stated, sadness in his voice. "I really think I should have married her." He had broken up with her when she was twenty-six. He had been the same age.

Because my client regretted his decision, he continued to date substitute Jessicas. Because the first Jessica wasn't actually replaceable, my client kept searching. After he decided to forgive himself, he cleared the pattern using Healing Streams of Grace. The last time I heard from this client, he was taking a break from dating altogether, which I think was probably a good idea. I felt certain that in the future he would date a more mature woman.

Resentments are challenging to work through because we might be embarrassed about admitting that we are resentful. We develop resentment when we think we have been treated unjustly, and perhaps we should have been given more praise, respect, love, or appreciation.

Resentment is particularly aggravating because it can lead to fantasies of revenge or establish a cycle of victim entitlement. If someone hurt or neglected us, it's natural to desire retribution. If we can't deliver a payback to the correct party, though, we might inflict our anger on someone else or even ourselves.

As well, when we feel victimized, we might think that the world owes us. Since we're not going to get what we want from the party that hurt us, we project our expectations on others. This is a lose-lose situation. When someone can't live up to our expectations, we'll feel disappointed. No one can fill a hole made by someone else.

I frequently search the Shadow Records for trauma or neglect if a client is continually resentful. Uncovering the original offenders and offenses supports a client in grieving the actual losses. At that point, my client can take actions that will lead toward real and self-responsible change.

For instance, I worked with a young man who wanted to be a college football player, but every time a scout watched him play, he flubbed up. It turned out that his father had never come to any of his football games. The young man resented the fact that a scout would pay more attention to his game than would his father. Once this young man grieved his father's lack of interest, he realized that the problem lay in his father, not with himself. The young player released the need to have his father show up. The next time a scout appeared at a game, my client played brilliantly.

The Book of Life
"GOD'S EYEGLASSES"

What if there were a way to see yourself through the eyes of the Spirit, or to wear "God's eyeglasses"? What might happen?

- Wisdom might replace regrets.
- Resentments could give way to an understanding of others' frailties, leading to a letting go.
- In place of festering wounds, misperceptions, stuck feelings, self-judgment, fear, and shame, what might stir but compassion, support, and love?

The Book of Life is an interactive library holding the Spirit's perceptions of us. Every being has their own Book of Life, which is a collection of the best ways to perceive all situations, thoughts, emotions, and events across time. What makes these perceptions the "best" is that they are based on higher truths, such as compassion and mercy.

Think about it. Frequently we feel stuck because we evaluate ourselves (or others) without mercy, defined as clemency or grace. Our heart is rusty, crusted with resentments and regrets because we don't pardon ourselves or others. We deny or repress our emotions because we can't imagine ourselves as deserving of an embrace. We hurt others or allow others to hurt us because we feel unworthy of charity. What's the antidote? The view available through the Book of Life, which I like to call "God's eyeglasses."

The Spirit's perceptions would never empower cruelty or evil but rather reveal ways to become loving and strong. Rather than enabling abuse or hatred, they would invoke forgiveness and security. In short, "God's eyeglasses" would release us from the past, plant us in the present, and open a loving future.

I work constantly to access the Book of Life in order to perceive situations the way that the Spirit would. In fact, I conduct my sessions as if wearing God's eyeglasses. In the journey shown next, you'll learn a particularly easy way to gain insight from the Book of Life, as well as the other two records.

A healing
–EXERCISE–

Journeying into the
Three Soul Records

In this three-part exercise you'll be guided into the three soul records: the Akashic Records, the Shadow Records, and the Book of Life. You'll start with Spirit-to-Spirit and be ushered into the records via the journeying technique presented in the previous chapter. You'll also integrate healing streams into your process to implement desirable change.

Before conducting this exercise, select an important issue. Choose a focus for a healing or a manifesting need, a long-held regret or resentment, or a negative pattern. You'll focus on the same issue within each library, thereby experiencing the capabilities of each. After you've acquainted yourself with the records, you can journey into any of them individually or collectively for any reason whenever you want.

STEP ONE: **Preparation.** Settle into a comfortable position and conduct Spirit-to-Spirit, affirming your spirit, others' spirits, and the Spirit. Select an issue you'd like to work through and establish an intention in regard to the outcome you would like. Know that the Spirit will ultimately bring about the optimum result.

STEP TWO: **Focus on Your Thymus.** Your thymus is the bodily site for your eighth chakra. Ask the Spirit to bring you into the center of this organ and activate your spirit within it. You'll find yourself on a shining white marble floor floating in the oceanic night, above which shine the bright stars. To your right is a door labeled "The Akashic Records." To your left is a door with a sign that reads "The Shadow Records."

STEP THREE: **Enter the Akashic Records.** Turn to the right door, open it, and pass through the subsequent hallway. Without leaving your thymus, you'll find yourself in the time-space that explains your issue's origination. Experience the situation that caused the challenging issue. Ask the Spirit to inform you about how the experience is still affecting you. You can also ask the Spirit to project you into the future that is most likely to occur if the issue continues to dominate your life. Then ask to perceive another possible future—one that might ensue should the situation change. If appropriate, ask the Spirit to alter the past or the concurrent reality, thus creating a storyline that would ensure the positive future. Finally, ask the Spirit to send Healing Streams of Grace to everyone involved with this issue.

Exit the Akashic Records when you feel ready and return to the marble floor.

STEP FOUR: **Enter the Shadow Records.** Enter the
doorway to the left. It is now time to figure out
if regrets or resentments play a role in your focal
issue.

You are surrounded in fog. The fog cleaves if
you do hold a regret, revealing the circumstances involved in your desire to have been different. Ask the Spirit to help you comprehend the
reasons you held onto the situation. When you
fully understand the dynamics, ask the Spirit to
reveal the wisdom you can gain from this experience and to send Healing Streams of Grace
to all concerned. When you've settled the issue,
the haze returns.

Now request that the Spirit expose any long-
held resentments. If they exist, the cloud splits
so you can view the experience causing resentment. Ask for support in owning the reasons
that you held onto the resentments. When you
understand your motivation, ask the Spirit to
send Healing Streams of Grace to you and others. These flow around and into you like shafts
of sunlight, clearing and healing. When finished,
thank the Spirit and exit the shadow realms by

walking through the doorway and returning to the marble floor in your thymus. If you didn't receive the full assistance needed, you certainly will during the following Book of Life exercise.

STEP FIVE: **Viewing Through the Book of Life.**

You are back in your thymus and standing upon the white marble tile. The doors to the Akashic and Shadow Records are closed.

A being appears in front of you. It indicates that it was sent by the Spirit and is therefore trustworthy. It holds a book, which it extends toward you.

You take the book. Words are imprinted upon it. These include your name and the title "The Book of Life." Peruse the book—the cover, texture, colors, feel, and aromas—and then open it. Nestled in between hollowed-out pages is a pair of eyeglasses.

You put on the eyeglasses; through them, review the issue bothering you. It plays out as if you're watching a play or movie; however, you perceive the situation through the eyes of the Spirit. As you watch the scene, you find yourself releasing the negativity or trauma held in regard to the situation. When you're left with only wisdom, put the glasses back in the book. Your spiritual companion closes the covers and takes the book, informing you that it will be returned when needed.

STEP SIX: **Close.** When ready, close your eyes and breathe deeply. Open your eyes again and become aware of your surroundings. The Spirit has lifted you out of your thymus and returned you to everyday reality.

* * * * * * *

Summary

There are three main energy libraries that store your soul's experiences. These are the Akashic Records, which hold events and perceptions from the potential and actual past, concurrent and actual present, and possible and most likely future times. The Shadow Records store what we wish could or should have happened. And finally, the Book of Life allows us to perceive situations as our higher self or the Spirit would see them. All of these mystical vehicles are available through journeying via the eighth chakra's bodily site, the thymus.

CHAPTER NINE

Trauma Recovery

Trauma recovery is frequently a painful and challenging process. After all, trauma is caused by injuries. As well, there are so many different causes and types of trauma that it can be hard to figure out the reasons for or nature of a trauma. Because of this, treating trauma can be complicated.

Regardless, freeing yourself from trauma is one of the most important tasks you can accomplish through energy work. Trauma causes long-term damage and frequently impedes progress. Fortunately, you've already learned about the subtle energy tool most apt to support a recovery from superficial, deep, acute, or chronic trauma. It's the Healing Streams of Grace, and they were introduced in chapter 4.

My personal take on trauma is that many therapeutic methods lack an important key: subtle energy. From an energetic perspective, trauma recovery necessitates tracking and clearing the forces involved in a physical, psychological, or spiritual injury. This "clearing of forces" can be effectively accomplished with Healing Streams of Grace and the understanding of how subtle energies create, sustain, and release trauma.

I begin this chapter by describing a few of the situations that can inflict trauma. Next, I describe "forces," the energetics you must comprehend to put Healing Streams of Grace to work. I then usher you through a guided journey that will show you how to apply the Healing Streams of Grace toward the healing of a personal trauma. Finally, I'll share a simple exercise that makes use of the healing streams and also the light wand technique introduced in chapter 6. Much good can be accomplished if you add these ideas to your medicine kit.

What Is Trauma?

THE MANY FACES OF DISMAY

Technically, a trauma is a disturbing event or experience. We tend to think of trauma as caused by physical events, but the truth is that nearly any painful situation or interaction can cause short- or long-term negative effects. And though we usually link trauma to interactions with an object or a person, the truth is that all sorts of situations can inflict trauma. For example, trauma can be caused in any of the following ways:

- Through a personal experience, such as being struck or burned physically or taken advantage of sexually. Factors increasing the seriousness of physical wounding include the use of drugs, alcohol, violence, and abuse.

- By witnessing a traumatic event affecting someone else, whether we know them or not, such as by observing abuse in our home, watching a video of a terrorist beheading, or witnessing a shooting.

- By spending time with someone who has been traumatized, such as a mother who was sexually abused or a father who barely survived a war.

- Through our family line, such as via the epigenetic material, the gene codes that hold our ancestors' memories, feelings, and reactions.

- By injuring ourselves either physically or emotionally.

- By inflicting trauma-causing wounds on another, whether a person or an animal.

- Psychological or emotional wounding, especially if intermittent or repetitive but also if singular and never addressed or validated.

Trauma Indicators

How do you know if you or another person is affected by trauma? Trauma is frequently affiliated with the following:

- Physical pains that are hard to heal
- Illnesses that can't be explained
- Insomnia and fatigue
- Nightmares
- Difficulties in concentrating
- Anxiety or depression
- Shock and denial
- Guilt and shame
- Withdrawal from normal life
- Addictions
- Lack of satisfying relationships
- Flashbacks and triggers
- Codependency
- Sadness and hopelessness

Of course, these symptoms can be caused by other factors, which is why it's important to consult a licensed professional if you think you are affected by trauma.

Although nearly everyone would feel bad if experiencing any of the above situations, trauma is actually more subjective than objective. The long-term effects are worse if a situation or series of events cause us to stop feeling safe or if we're left feeling alone or helpless. The most challenging of situations includes those which are unexpected, involve intentional cruelty, and occur in childhood.

As well, there are often overlooked causes of trauma. These include the following interactions:

- Neglect
- Sexual abuse, overt and covert
- Physical abuse, overt and covert
- Exposure to addictions and abuse
- Emotional abuse
- Verbal abuse
- Psychological abuse
- Spiritual abuse (fanaticism, brainwashing, terrorism, shaming)
- Bullying
- Separation from a parent
- Unstable or unsafe environment
- Financial loss
- Intensive medical procedures

- Falls or sports injuries
- Surgery, especially in first three years of life
- Sudden death of someone close
- Auto accident
- Significant breakup
- Humiliation or embarrassing event
- Discovery of a life-debilitating illness or problem in self or other

The Relationship of Subtle Energy to Trauma
A MATTER OF FORCE

Most of us understand why it's so damaging to undergo personal trauma, but we might question why we are affected long-term. We might also wonder why we're so impacted by observing rather than being involved in a traumatic situation. One explanation lies in the nature of subtle energy.

As we've established, subtle energy underlies physical reality. Damage happens when harmful subtle energies are introduced or forced into our body, mind, or soul. We can handle subtle energies that match our own, but when the subtle energies *don't* complement our own, these mismatched energies create a disturbance.

Trauma is incurred when the subtle energies involved in an event are organized as a force, or a wave of charged energy. A force can be a natural energy (such as wind or water), a physical energy (such as a field emanating from an object or person), an emotional energy (which can be delivered through an expressed or unexpressed feeling), a verbal energy (which might be an internal or external statement or a stated or unstated belief), a relational energy (which is created when two or more beings are sharing space), a spiritual energy (which involves beliefs about one's spiritual nature, birthright, or the Spirit), or other types of subtle energies, such as energies emitted from a soul or entity, carried in from past lives, or generated by epigenetic material or the environment. Basically, almost any energetic interaction can formulate a force.

A force isn't in and of itself a good or bad thing, but it's one thing to have the wind play with your hair or feel the trickling of water from a spring rain. It's quite another to be caught in a tornado or have your house washed away by a tsunami. Usually, the stronger the force affecting us, the stronger the effect. As well, the more mismatched the force in relation to our energetic signature, the more traumatic and long-term the impact.

It's hard, if not sometimes impossible, to perceive a force. Mainly we notice a force's effect. Someone gets hit and we spy the welt or broken bone. A kid gets yelled at and we feel bad when they cry. We certainly don't perceive the subtle energetic charges carried on the force, such as the abuser's anger or the beliefs causing an alcoholic to drive intoxicated. All we really know is that there is an adverse effect to a situation.

Unfortunately, few physicians or therapists know how to track and analyze the subtle energies and forces lodged within or affecting a victim. Rather, they note trauma symptoms, such as those listed in the previous section. And even if the traumatized individual knows the origin of the trauma, they seldom know how many charges are locked into their system, all of which linger long after the originating event. We can use energy work to track and clear these charges, as well as the forces they are carried on, and also to repair the energetic wounds.

Think about it: the fact that subtle energetic charges are carried by forces explains why energies can get stuck in our body, mind, or soul for nearly forever. Basically these charges can be physical, psychological, or spiritual. This explanation of trauma also reveals the reason why we can witness a negative situation and end up affected. Quite simply, the charges carried on the invisible forces generated by the traumatic interaction are transmitted to everyone around. The charges that don't suit us can damage us.

When performing energy work on oneself or another, there are several factors to consider. Following is a more precise description of what actually occurs from an energetic point of view when we're traumatized. This outline will reveal the keys involved in working energetically to recover from trauma.

The Path of Trauma
THE FACTORS INVOLVED

Trauma-causing forces engage in the body in the following ways:

Origination

It can be important to know what or who generated the adverse force, but sometimes a traumatized person doesn't know the origin of a source. You can still aid in trauma recovery without this knowledge because energy work involves examining a trauma by searching for the intrusive force or its side effects.

Entry Point

A force enters the victim through some part of their subtle or physical body, such as the auric field, chakras, or bodily tissue. A soul can also carry a negative force from one lifetime to another. When this is the case, the force still enters the person or being through some part of the subtle or physical body. Entrance points usually exhibit symptoms of one sort or another—physical, psychological, or spiritual.

Exit Point

Most of the time a force exits, or in the case of ricocheting wounds, creates multiple exits. These exit points usually display symptoms that might be the same or different than those at the entrance points.

Pathway

The force carves a pathway through the subtle energy system and body. The following can occur along this pathway, either right after the force enters the system or over time:

- *Pathway remains empty.* The pathway can remain clear, in which case the functions both subtle and physical linked to the pathway might be adversely affected.

- *Lodged forces.* Not all forces exit. Those that remain locked in a part of the body or energetic system form congestion and related physical and emotional pain.
- *Pathway fills.* The pathway can fill in with mismatched energies.
- *Charges linger.* The charges carried in on the harmful force can remain in the pathway and attract traumas that mirror the original trauma.
- *Heals.* The pathway can be filled with beneficial energies that enable healing.

Wounded Self

The self injured by the force goes into shock and can become stuck. This concept is explained next.

Trauma and the Wounded Self

Trauma creates a wounded self. I want to explain what this means from an energetic viewpoint.

When we're struck with a force, our biological programming sends us into shock. My research has convinced me that the thalamus, an organ in the brain, is in charge of this process. Energetically, shock appears like a bubble that surrounds the aggrieved self.

Shock is a vital survival mechanism. As long as we're ensconced in this subtle energy container, we won't feel pain or fear. We can react to a threat without the limitations of emotional or physical anguish. As a threat subsides, the shock wave is supposed to disintegrate, at which point we start feeling our emotions and physical reactions. If someone assists us with this process, the wounds caused by the force will heal, as will our feelings and body, and we can progress in life.

If our traumatized self remains enfolded in the shock bubble, however, we can't recover. The wounded aspect remains stuck and can't mature or progress. The forces can't clear or heal either. The locked-in forces shift our tensegrity, or structural balance, throwing off different parts of our system. Most of these symptoms will occur at the force's entrance and exit points, along the pathway, or where the energetics are lodged. As well, the imprisoned self will continue to remain hidden or every so often hijack the maturing self, throwing us into post-traumatic stress symptoms, such as flashbacks and triggers.

As implied, there are many steps necessary for energetic trauma recovery. These are as follows:

- Locating and healing entry, exits, or lodged forces.

- Cleaning out and appropriately filling in pathways.
- Clearing the thalamus.
- Rescuing and reintegrating the shocked self.

How do we accomplish these goals? We use Healing Streams of Grace, as you'll experience in the following exercise.

Journey for Trauma Recovery

This exercise walks you though the steps necessary for trauma recovery by addressing the subtle energy concerns. These include isolating the subtle energies that originally created or have since locked in or further substantiated the trauma and its lingering effects.

What should you do if you have difficulty obtaining information in any of the steps involved in this exercise? First, be gentle with yourself. Traumas can be extraordinarily challenging to clear. The very nature of trauma is that it's painful. An aspect of the self might resist uncovering the deepest of wounds, betrayals, or emotional residue. As well, working with trauma energetically might be new to you. Naturally, this might make the following steps confusing or clunky. If you feel blocked at any stage of this exercise, you can ask for healing streams, take a time out, and return to it later or ask for a sign to help you obtain the desired data. You might also consider working with a professional healer or therapist. The presence of another person greatly enhances the effectiveness of trauma relief. If the latter suggestion feels right to you, know that this exercise was successful even if you didn't complete it. It got you to the point of opening for assistance.

STEP ONE: **Preparation.** Find a quiet place in which to conduct this exercise. You can perform it as an internal guided exercise or use a paper and pencil to write down your observations.

STEP TWO: **Create a Focus.** Pinpoint a trauma site or experience you would like to clear. You don't need to know what actually caused the trauma or when it occurred. For instance, you might have a chronically sore elbow and want to discover what created the pain. You might experience a bothersome emotional reaction. As best as you can, fashion an intention statement. You can make it specific or general, such as, "I would like to track and heal the causes of my sore elbow" or "I am clearing the emotional imprints of being in a car accident."

STEP THREE: **Conduct Spirit-to-Spirit.** Run through Spirit-to-Spirit, first affirming your spirit, others' spirits, and then affirming the Spirit. Trust the Spirit with your intention, knowing that the Spirit might change or evolve your goal.

STEP FOUR: **Locate the Entry Point.** All traumas have an entry point. Ask the Spirit to pinpoint the original entry point for the trauma you're focusing on. You might visualize it in your mind, hear words describing it, or feel a sensation or emotions in your body or a chakra, or even sense a spot in the auric field. Now ask the Spirit to inform you about the situation causing this wounding. Spend as much time on this step as needed.

STEP FIVE: **Follow the Pathway.** Intuitively track the pathway forged by the invading force. As you do this, become aware of the energy of the force. Did it originate as a natural, physical, emotional, spiritual, or another type of force? Request that the Spirit help you discern if there is an exit point or multiple exit points or if the force became lodged. Also evaluate the state of the pathway: is it clear, clogged, or otherwise inhabited? Remain in this assessment phase as long as needed.

STEP SIX: **Request Healing.** Ask that the Spirit provide the healing steams of grace needed to clear and fill the entrance point, the pathway, and the exit point. Know that the streams required will remain connected as long as necessary and will shift over time.

STEP SEVEN: **Find the Wounded Self.** Ask the Spirit to help you perceive the wounded self, who is held within a bubble formed of shock waves. Spend as much time as needed relating to this self. You might hear, feel, or touch this self. Ask it to relate its story and feelings. Most important, ask the Spirit to fully attend to this self's needs, even while it's in the bubble.

STEP EIGHT: **Clear the Shock and Thalamus.** Now request that the Spirit generate Healing Streams of Grace to clear the thalamus and to use as replacements for the shock waves. This enclosure of grace will assure that the wounded self processes grief in a healthy way.

STEP NINE: **Ask for Insight.** Ask the Spirit to provide you any additional insight or knowledge about how to reengage with life.

STEP TEN: **Close.** When ready, take a few deep breaths, affirm the Spirit, and return to your everyday life.

Using the Light Wand on Trauma

The light wand serves as a simple and quick way to help clear a traumatic force. It is most effective if you've already conducted the previous exercise and know where the entrance wound is. It is also a fantastic process to use if you've just incurred a wound; for instance, you just hit your head on something. Primarily you'll be pointing your "light wand" finger/s at the entrance wound and sending Healing Streams of Grace through it.

With a physical injury, especially one just received, it's pretty easy to figure out the entrance wound. If you stubbed your toe, you'll direct the light wand—a finger or set of multiple fingers—at the toe. But it can be hard to discern the entrance wound of a long-term ache or pain or a psychological or spiritual malady.

What can you do if you're confused? You can always use Spirit-to-Spirit and ask the Spirit to tell or show you the location of the entrance wound. Another option is to mentally figure out the entrance wound for a trauma. Track a painful site to the nearest chakra and point the finger/s at the chakra. You can also relate an emotional or spiritual symptom to a chakra. Use the chakra information in chapter 1 to link a problem to the obvious chakra. For instance, a "broken heart" that started in a failed romance involves your fourth chakra.

It can be hard to differentiate the entrance and exit wounds. Some clients only display symptoms at the exit wound. If you can't tell, ask the Spirit to help you implement change through the exit wound.

As for the actual process, employ the technique as you were shown in chapter 6. Simply direct the finger/s at the entrance wound and ask the Spirit to send through Healing Streams of Grace. Remain focused until you sense the streams are busily at work.

* * * * * * *

Summary

Recovery from trauma can be a long and involved process. Trauma, which can be caused by any number of events, involves the penetration of energetic forces. Pertinent entrance and exit points, as well as the pathway, can be repaired to encourage trauma recovery. It's also important to rescue the traumatized self, which might be encapsulated in a bubble of shock and unable to function.

CHAPTER TEN

The Four Zones of the Soul

Many life issues originate in the soul. As simple as this statement is, the concept is complicated. After all, our soul has journeyed nearly everywhere and "everywhen." Fortunately, there are four main zones, or planes of existence, that the soul experiences in regard to a single lifetime. Knowing about these zones and the types of issues you can work through points you to the origin of a soul-based challenge.

In this chapter I first acquaint you with the four stages that a soul journeys through in a single lifetime. The purpose is to help you analyze these zones in terms of your current life. By focusing Spirit-to-Spirit and Healing Streams of Grace on the applicable zone, you can make substantial changes in your life. The exercise at the end of this chapter will guide you through each zone so you can check each one out and return to any of them at a later date.

The Four Soul Zones

We know that life is complicated. To help us better understand what our life is supposed to be like, therapists organize our development in stages. If we have an issue, we can use this information to track a challenge back to its originating stage and "fill in the holes." We can perform the same operation by examining the four developmental stages a soul passes through during every incarnation. I also call these stages the "zones of existence."

In general, the first zone occurs before conception, the second zone happens during embryonic development, the third zone actives right after birth and relates to the overall lifetime, and the doorway into the final zone is available when the body is dying or after death. We can access any of these zones anytime, however, which is what I do if a client is dealing with certain critical issues, whether physical, psychological, or spiritual.

What are these four zones and their related issues? Let's take a look.

Zone One: The White Zone

Before conception, the soul enters the white zone to negotiate a soul contract. I call this arena the "white zone" because it psychically looks like a big white room to me.

A soul contract works like all business contracts in that it lays out what is going to happen and when. The caveat is that the terms relate to an upcoming life. Through the negotiation process, we forge agreements with many of the souls (people, animals, and guides) we will interact with during the upcoming life. We also select major events, such as accidents, career paths, diseases, romantic relationships, and other life situations. I call these preselected desires "destiny points." Only specific events are decreed; life dictates its own terms. Typically, a soul contract isolates situations that will help us work through our karma, or spiritual lessons. We arrive at this contract with the help of the Spirit or a specialized guide.

All sorts of problems originate in the white zone—or, rather, during life because of the white zone. In a nutshell, the original contract agreements might not be operational or beneficial or even able to be fulfilled. Life is chaotic. Events might unfold (or not) that make it impossible to fulfill a destiny point. I'll give you a few examples, all of which I've seen with my clients.

Imagine that you decided to be childless in order to learn how to self-parent, but then you changed your mind in adulthood. You might now have difficulties getting pregnant. Pretend that you preselected a certain set of parents and then your mother-to-be married the "wrong" man. Consequently, you are plagued with a sense of depression that you can't decipher.

Other common mishaps relate to romance.

Romance frequently begins in the clouds. In the white zone we might agree to meet and date, marry, and even divorce another soul. These predestined agreements are replete with problems. Sometimes the penultimate partner fails to appear. Other times the "soul mate" is unlikable or might reject us. I've even seen situations in which the desirable "other" didn't even incarnate.

Soul plans often fail to match reality. Because of this, I help individuals visit the white zone if there are situations that are really "off," if they sense an empty space that is "supposed" to be filled, or when they can't make peace with what has or hasn't happened. The goal is to update the negative parts of our soul plan and thus change our life circumstances.

Zone Two: The Gray Zone

After conception, our soul departs the white zone and hurtles through the gray zone, which separates the white zone and the body. The soul usually doesn't enter the body until well into the second trimester or even at birth.

Rather, the soul hovers around the body after passing through the gray zone, interacting with guides and visiting with the parents-to-be.

The gray zone is essentially a void that erases past life memories. The gray energy within it causes a sort of soul amnesia in relation to past and in-between lives. Our current soul contract remains intact, but we forget about it. With our memories obliterated, we can deal with situations with fresh eyes. (Memories are reawakened again after death and can often be retrieved through journeying.)

There are many issues that can arise because of the gray zone. These primarily involve entity attachment and memory challenges.

Entities frequently linger in the gray zone, souls that were formerly incarnated on earth and souls from other planets and dimensions. Those looking for an "easy way" into the world can attach to an incoming soul, consequently shifting the soul's destiny or causing interference. Sometimes a dark force can even prevent a soul from incarnating completely, which can cause dissociation and even pathological responses to life. For instance, the interfering soul might "steer the ship," causing sociopathic-type behaviors.

Also, the memory erasing can create problems. If too many remembrances or patterns are erased, the incoming soul might be overly naïve and vulnerable to manipulative people or beings. Sometimes there is an incomplete erasure and former memories can interfere with the current destiny. As an example, I once worked with a young girl who recalled being buried alive in Greece. She was constantly visited by night terrors as sheer darkness triggered the horror of dying in the dark. Once we helped her process the memory, she began sleeping like a baby.

Bottom line, I examine the gray zone if someone seems lost and overly naïve, pathologically undeveloped, has felt a presence haunting them since they were young, or experience unnecessary or intrusive memories from the past.

Zone Three: The Red Zone

The red zone is comparable to an extra energy body that runs alongside the physical body. It is similar to an auric layer in that it exists outside of the physical body and is composed of subtle energy. As compared to an auric layer, however, it is thicker and more dense. It is also activated just before or during birth, as are the auric layers. However, it is not linked to a chakra, as is an individual auric field.

This energy body is like a "gas tank" that magically refills in order to provide life energy to the subtle and physical body. The fuel is comprised of subtle elements from the environment, which are converted to a vital energy that stokes both subtle and physical structures.

There are many problems that can occur with the red zone. These include blockages caused by family programs, attachments to beings that steal our red zone energy, and an absorption of others' psychic energies. When the latter occurs, there is no room for the incoming subtle elements. Problems with the red zone frequently present as severe fatigue, lack of energy, or any of the conditions that involve these symptoms, such as fibromyalgia or chronic fatigue.

Zone Four: The Black Zone

Nearly every culture wonders what happens after we die. One opportunity we're given either right before or after we die is entrance into the black zone.

I perceive the black zone as a meeting space in which we visit with all the souls that we've connected to when alive. This space is sacred ground. The purpose of gathering is to bestow forgiveness.

We can only answer for our own soul. It is here that we can ask forgiveness from others, give it to others, and grant it to ourselves. Even if others have already passed or are alive, an aspect of their soul is invited to the meeting.

While this zone is mainly available to the dying or just-deceased, it can be visited anytime. I guide individuals into this zone if they are struggling with forgiveness issues of any sort. For instance, I often work with individuals who were abused and can't find it in their heart to forgive the abuser. The goal isn't to make the previous abuse okay; rather, it's to release the energetic attachments that inevitably form between the victim and the abuser.

Another major forgiveness theme is self-forgiveness. I often find that it's harder for people to forgive their own negative actions than to release others from their harmful behavior. Ultimately, grace is about mercy, a gift that we must give others but also ourselves.

Journey into the Four Zones of the Soul

This guided meditation will help you access each of your four soul zones. In this journey, conducted within your thymus in accordance with the style introduced in chapter 7, you'll remain open to whatever the Spirit wants to show you in each zone. After you've conducted this journey, you can quickly slip into any of the four zones at a later time with a particular intention.

STEP ONE: **Conduct Spirit-to-Spirit.** Find a quiet, comfortable place and conduct Spirit-to-Spirit. Affirm your own spirit, others' spirits, and the Spirit.

STEP TWO: **Center in Your Eighth Chakra.** Ask the Spirit to guide you into the bodily site for your eighth chakra, which is your thymus. Become aware of the darkly lit ocean of energy around you and the twinkling of beautiful stars above you. Standing upon a glistening white floor, you can perceive four hallways at the same equidistance as are the directions on a compass. Each of these short pathways ends with a door. They are labeled with the four names of the zones: *White Zone, Gray Zone, Red Zone,* and *Black Zone.*

STEP THREE: **Visit the White Zone.** With the Spirit accompanying you, enter the white zone. You find yourself in a white room. A spiritual guide sits at a white table and points to a chair on the other side of the table. You take a seat.

The guide sets a contract on the table and rifles through it before showing you a page that you need to see. The guide points out a passage, which you read. The guide then explains the pertinent information and why you might want to rewrite this passage. With the guide's assistance, you alter this passage, after which the Spirit seals the contract with Healing Streams of Grace. Healing streams are also provided to support the resulting transformation. When ready, exit the white zone and return to the center of your thymus.

STEP FOUR: **Enter the Gray Zone**. You enter the doorway marked *Gray Zone* and find yourself in a swirling gray fog. The Spirit surrounds you in a bubble made of Healing Streams of Grace to keep you safely cocooned in light.

The Spirit points out the challenges that started affecting you in the gray zone. Are there attachments? Memories that should have or shouldn't have been erased? Allow the Spirit to send you the Healing Streams of Grace required to address any concerns, and then exit the gray zone, returning to the center of your thymus.

STEP FIVE: **Assess the Red Zone.** It's time to walk through the doorway labeled *Red Zone*. You find yourself in an office, which is the control room for the red zone. There is a desk in front of you. You sit in the desk chair and turn on the computer monitor on the desk.

On the monitor appears an image of your body, which is surrounded by a layer of red. This is your red zone. The Spirit helps you examine this zone, showing you where it's too thick, too thin, creased, or otherwise disturbed. You also check for attachments, holes, and puncture wounds, as well as areas that leak vital energy or hold unhealthy energy. The Spirit also points out which subtle elements are entering the zone from the environment and which are blocked.

After completing your assessment, allow the Spirit to guide you in making changes in your red zone by using your mouse and watching the monitor. As the zone is repaired, you'll observe the transformation on the screen but also feel the alterations. When finished, subtle energies will be flowing freely into your red zone, converting into life energy for your physical and subtle bodies. Sit back and invite Healing Streams of Grace into and through your body, mind, and soul. These lock in the red zone changes. Exit this zone when you are ready.

STEP SIX: **Touchdown in the Black Zone.** There is one more door to walk through. It is labeled *Black Zone*. With the Spirit as your companion, enter this zone through the center of your thymus. This is a realm in which anything is possible if one is merciful.

Every soul that you've met or will meet in this lifetime is present. Ask the Spirit to show you if there is a soul requiring forgiveness. As this information becomes clear, allow the Spirit to guide you through the necessary process. Then ask if there is anyone you need to request forgiveness from. The Spirit delivers your request. Whether or not the party agrees to forgive you, you can forgive yourself for the ways you've infringed upon others. Ask what change you have to commit to, and then, finally, check to see if there is a need to self-forgive. Request assistance from the Spirit if you need it. Know that all forgiveness is delivered through the Healing Streams of Grace delivered by the Spirit to all concerned parties. The bond between the Spirit and the forgiven is strengthened as mercy is delivered.

When finished with the black zone, return to the center of your thymus.

STEP SEVEN: **Closing.** Bask in the sense of renewal and joy, then ask the Spirit to return you to your everyday life with love and grace.

* * * * * * *

Summary

There are four stages, or zones, that a soul goes through in relation to a specific life. These are the white zone, in which the soul creates a soul plan for that lifetime; the gray zone, which washes away past life memories; the red zone, an energy layer in the auric field that converts subtle elements to life energy; and the black zone, a state available for making peace with others. You can journey into any of these zones to release pertinent issues and access related gains.

Conclusion

One of my favorite authors is John Muir, who advised the following:

"Climb the mountains and get their good tidings. Nature's peace will flow into you as sunshine flows into trees" (Muir 56).

The goal of performing energy work, the art of directing physical and subtle energies, is to enable a continual basking in the sunshine of life. In fact, the actual rays of the sun are comparable to the Healing Streams of Grace available to anyone for any reason. Like blessings, these streams of energy, emanating from the Creator, are vehicles for healing and manifesting.

We access the streams using Spirit-to-Spirit, the most universal of techniques. By affirming your own spirit, others' spirits, and the greater Spirit, you center in your best self. You highlight the highest aspects of others and connect yourself directly to the most holy one of all. Within the safe cocoon of Spirit-to-Spirit, you can invite healing, open to manifestations, and receive spiritual guidance.

One of the reasons that I highlighted Muir's quote is that it emphasizes the goodness of nature. In this book's pages you learned about the most fundamental essences of the natural world, the eleven subtle elements that compose all of reality. By continually working with these elements, you can balance yourself and others physically, psychologically, and spiritually. There's no easier tool for this task than the light wand, a method for directing subtle energies, such as Healing Streams of Grace and the subtle elements, through something as normal as one of your fingers.

Muir's quotation speaks of the need to climb a mountain. You don't actually have to do this to avail yourself of the signature energy work techniques and processes described in this book. But you might need to journey into the various mystical dimensions that hold the secrets to health and happiness. Travel at will into the different libraries of your soul, including the Akashic Records, which store the past, present, and future; the Shadow Records, which resonate with what could or should have happened; and the Book of Life, the lens that enables a god-view of yourself and others.

Employing the simple journeying technique included here can also take you in another direction, through the four zones of your soul. Every lifetime our soul visits the white zone, where it establishes a contract for the upcoming incarnation. After establishing a soul contract, it then hurdles through the gray zone, in which foggy clouds wipe out our soul's past life memories so we can start anew. At birth the red zone is activated, and we receive a continual flow of subtle elements that fuel the body toward the soul's desires. And then, at the end of life, the soul touches into the black zone, the meeting ground designed to encourage forgiveness and release.

As I shared in the introduction, I use every technique in this book on a daily basis, both personally and professionally. I continually delve into the elements, soul records, and zones to assist myself and others. Not only do these, my signature processes and techniques, enable me to fully support others, but they support me in living a life in the most natural of ways. I climb life's mountains, but I also rest in the valleys. I drink in sunshine from dawn to dusk. I live fully, which is essentially what we're all on this good green earth to do.

The Essential Energy Work Techniques

Here are the quick and easy steps needed to perform my signature techniques Spirit-to-Spirit and Healing Streams of Grace.

Spirit-to-Spirit

This easy three-step process centers you in your essential self, allows you to interact with the highest aspect of others, and turns your will over to a greater power. By using this technique, you invite only the best outcomes for self and others.

- Affirm your personal spirit.
- Affirm others' spirits, those seen and unseen.
- Affirm the Spirit, which works toward the highest outcome for all concerned.

Healing Streams of Grace

Healing streams of grace pour endlessly from the Spirit. Once energetically connected to you or another, these streams will bring about the highest possible outcome. This promise relates to healing, manifesting, or obtaining guidance.

Following are simple steps for requesting the universal streams for self or other.

- Conduct Spirit-to-Spirit.
- Ask the Spirit to send the correct Healing Streams of Grace to self or another. These can also be beamed into an object, substance, or anything else.
- Thank the Spirit for updating or changing these streams on an as-needed basis.

BIBLIOGRAPHY

Center for Spirituality & Healing at the University of Minnesota. "What Impact Does the Environment Have on Us?" http://www.takingcharge.csh.umn.edu/explore-healing-practices/healing-environment/what-impact-does-environment-have-us.

Collins, Danica. November 11, 2011. Underground Health Reporter. "Extraordinary Healing Power of Love... Causes Cancer to Vanish." www.underground healthreporter.com/bracohealing-power-of-love-cancer/.

Cornerstone Books. "Phineas Parkhurst Quimby." http://phineasquimby.wwwhubs.com/.

Cymascope. "Introduction." http://www.cymascope.com/cyma_research/history.html.

Emspak, Jesse. March 15, 2013. "Spooky! Quantum Action is 10,000 Faster Than Light." http://www.livescience.com/27920-quantum-action-faster-than-light.html.

Kamp, Matthias. Bruno Groning Circle of Friends. "Bruno Groning—A Revolution in Medicine." https://www.bruno-groening.org/en/bruno-groening/teachings/the-teaching-of-bruno-groening.

Muir, John. *Our National Parks*. New York: Houghton, Mifflin and Company, 1901.

Newton, Alonzo Eliot. *The Modern Bethesda, or, The Gift of Healing Restored*. New York: Newton Publishing, 1879. https://ia802604.us.archive.org/31/items/modern bethesdaor00newtrich/modernbethesdaor00newtrich.pdf.

Orzel, Chaz. January 20, 2010. Uncertain Principles. "Seven Essential Elements of Quantum Physics." http://scienceblogs.com/principles/2010/01/20 /seven-essential-elements-of-qu/.

Pearsall, Paul. *The Heart's Code: Tapping the Wisdom and Power of Our Heart Energy*. New York: Broadway Books, 1998.

Twin Pregnancies and Beyond. "Vanishing Twin Syndrome." http://www.twin-pregnancy-and-beyond .com/vanishing-twin.html.

Walia, Arjun. September 27, 2014. "Nothing Is Solid & Everything Is Energy—Scientists Explain the World of Quantum Physics." www.collective-evolution.com /2014/09/27/this-is-the-world-of-quantum-physics -nothing-is-solid-and-everything-is-energy/.

West, Brandon. April 16, 2014. "Proof that the Human Body is a Projection of Consciousness." http://www .wakingtimes.com/2014/04/16/proof-human-body -projection-consciousness/.

World Research Foundation. "Dr. James Rogers Newton… and His Gift of Healing." www.wrf.org/men-women -medicine/dr-james-newton-healing-gift.php.